ALL CHURCHES GREAT AND SMALL

ALL CHURCHES GREAT AND SMALL
The Church Scene in the United Kingdom

C. Peter Collinson

OM
publishing

First published in 1998 by OM Publishing

O4 03 02 01 00 99 98   7 6 5 4 3 2 1

OM Publishing is an imprint of Paternoster Publishing,
P.O. Box 300, Carlisle, Cumbria, CA3 0QS, U.K.
http://www.paternoster-publishing.com

British Library Cataloguing in Publication Data
A catalogue record for this book is available from the British Library.

ISBN 1-85078-311-X

Cover design by Mainstream, Lancaster
Typeset by WestKey Ltd, Falmouth, Cornwall
Printed in Great Britain by Mackays of Chatham PLC, Kent

To Kathleen, God's gift to me,
to whom I owe more than I can say

Contents

Introduction

The title of this book is not strictly accurate. It would have been next to impossible to have included every possible church. Nevertheless, nearly all are included under one heading or another. As a rule of thumb, to be included has meant that a church or denomination has a membership of at least a thousand. It also has a belief in the Trinity, although some who do not have that belief are included at the end of the book.

It has been necessary to hunt far and wide to assemble the information needed. I am extremely indebted to officials of churches and organisations, and others, who have responded to my queries, some going far beyond the line of duty. My aim has been to be as objective and authoritative as possible, whilst writing in a straightforward manner. I may not always have succeeded, and if so, I apologise. But I have been conscious of having to break new ground.

It is remarkable that, although books abound on world religions and on cults and new religious movements, not much at all has been published on Christian churches. Because of this, Christians often know little about churches other than their own — and sometimes not a lot about their own! Also, many misconceptions go the rounds. More than once, in my role as a Baptist minister, I have been informed by a stranger, 'Baptists are followers of John the Baptist, aren't they?' But then I myself have to admit that I used to carry round wrong ideas about certain churches. Most of us probably have done the same.

Hopefully, this book will help to put things right to some extent. But, in addition to that, I hope readers will be as fascinated as I have been to browse in front of this rich tapestry. We may be startled at times! But there is something very stimulating to catch a glimpse of where people come from in their understanding of the Church, and perhaps where they are going.

I have not included any of the hundreds of para-church organisations. Most do a wonderful job, but it would have been invidious to mention some and not others. I have tried simply to give a kind of snapshot of the churches themselves.

Neither have I mentioned aspects of church life which are common to most churches, e.g. youth and children's work. As much as anything, the emphasis is mainly on the distinctives, that which marks them out in their history, their beliefs and their practice. Some are more distinctive than others!

It needs to be remembered that membership figures are not necessarily a guide to church attendance. Sometimes attendance is more than the membership figures, sometimes less. It usually depends on how easy it is to become a member. The membership figures are taken from the *U.K. Christian Handbook Religious Trends No 1*, to which I am greatly indebted.

The first section, A Bird's-eye View, is an attempt to look at the church scene as a whole, giving a summary of major Christian beliefs, of the way denominations arose, of the way churches are governed, and perhaps most important of all, where Christians across the denominations get authority for their beliefs and practices. This last is becoming a burning issue.

Apart from this section's value in its own right, it can be a help when reading about the churches themselves. If a reader is not sure what certain words signify — words like 'liberal', 'evangelical', 'Arminian', 'ecumenical', they can refer back to this first section, where that word is defined and explained. The page number is in brackets following the word.

My earnest hope and prayer is that God would give us a greater understanding of one another, and continue to build his Church for his glory.

PART 1

A Bird's-eye View of Christian Churches

If birds could read, it would not be surprising if, flying over one of our big cities, one became quite confused as it saw a variety of church buildings, and an even greater variety of names on the noticeboards outside. Why? Why could they not all call themselves simply a Christian Church? Another bird might try to enlighten it, but in fact could make it even more confused because almost everything this other bird said was based on hearsay, much of it untrue.

As we attempt to dispel the confusion and misconception which seems everywhere today, it may be helpful first of all to take a flight ourselves to look at the whole scene, to take a bird's-eye view.

The situation today

Christianity is more widespread throughout the world than any other religion, and it is reckoned that more people have become Christians in the twentieth century than in all the other centuries put together. The increase has been chiefly in the developing world. Some 1900 million people would see themselves as Christians, about a third of the world's population. Few people would doubt that Christianity has had more impact on the history of the world than any other religion.

In Britain, secular writers tell us that Christianity is a spent force, that nobody goes to church any more. It may surprise them to know that over four million people in the UK attend Sunday services, more than go to football matches every week; even in 'pagan' England, over three million go to church every Sunday. Many individual churches have congregations of hundreds, some over a thousand. At the same time, it has to be admitted that overall the trend has been downward. This is not now as steep as it was, and there are grounds for thinking that before long the trend might be reversed.

Shared beliefs

Differences of belief exist among the churches, and this book shows that clearly. But it is also true that a great many foundational beliefs are shared by them all. The most important shared belief is that Jesus Christ is unique, that he is both man and God. This is the most important difference between mainline churches and what are often called cults and new religious movements. Cults are often vastly different from one another, but the common factor is that they do not believe in the Godhead of Jesus.

The Bible is the book which is basic for all Christian belief. Most churches accept its authority, although some go beyond it. The Old Testament (or Old Covenant) gives the Law of God and prophesies that a Messiah, 'anointed king', would come to deliver God's people. The New Testament declares that Jesus is the fulfilment of that prophecy, God coming as a human being.

At the age of 30 (he was probably born between 6 BC and 4 BC), he began his 3 year period of preaching and teaching about the kingdom of God. He did not see himself as a political deliverer, which was the popular idea of what the Messiah would be. He had not come to save Jews from the Romans, but people from their sins. He called for repentance, and warned of judgment. He proclaimed the characteristics of those who were truly members of God's kingdom. However, as distinct from other religions, it is not the teaching he gave as the founder of Christianity that is most significant. Christianity is centred in him as a person, especially in his death and resurrection. Through his death comes forgiveness for sins, and his resurrection guarantees eternal life. It is through him alone that fellowship with God can be enjoyed. He is the mediator between God and man.

The Bible also sees him as the great example of how to live, and as Lord of every Christian's life. They must aim to love God with their whole being, and to love their neighbours as themselves, showing kindness, forgiveness, humility and patience. This can only be accomplished with the enabling of the Holy Spirit, who is given to each true believer.

It is these basic truths which most churches believe. At different times, various summaries of these truths have been composed. The most well-known are the Apostles' and the Nicene creeds. In the mainline churches throughout the world, the Nicene is the most widely accepted. Most of this dates from AD 325. (The Apostles' Creed is used in the Western churches, but not in the Eastern churches.) The Nicene Creed states:

> We believe in one God, the Father, the almighty, maker of heaven and earth, of all that is, seen and unseen.
> We believe in one Lord, Jesus Christ, the only Son of God, eternally begotten of the Father, God from God, Light from

Light, true God from true God, begotten, not made, of one
Being with the Father. Through him all things were made.
For us men and our salvation, he came down from heaven;
by the power of the Holy Spirit he became incarnate of the
Virgin Mary, and was made man. For our sake, he was
crucified under Pontius Pilate; he suffered death and was
buried. On the third day, he rose again in accordance with
the Scriptures; he ascended into heaven and is seated at the
right hand of the Father. He will come again in glory to judge
the living and the dead, and his kingdom will have no end.

We believe in the Holy Spirit, the Lord, the giver of life, who
proceeds from the Father and the Son. With the Father and
the Son he is worshipped and glorified. He has spoken
through the prophets.

We believe in one holy catholic [meaning 'universal'] and
apostolic Church. We acknowledge one baptism for the forgiveness of sins. We look for the resurrection of the dead and
the life of the world to come.

Thus, the common belief is that there is only one God,
who has revealed himself as three Persons: the Father, the
Son and the Holy Spirit, known together as the Trinity.
There are not three Gods but one. The Father, the Son and
the Holy Spirit are each God, and together they are the one
God.

The growth of the churches

Under the leadership of the Apostles (the first disciples of
Jesus), groups of Christians formed churches. Each believer became a member by being baptised in water. They
met together regularly to worship God, and to be in-
structed in the Christian life. In the 'Lord's Supper' (Communion service), they ate bread and drank wine,

commemorating the death and resurrection of Jesus. They cared for each other, and preached the gospel to others.

In a short time, Christianity spread throughout the Roman Empire, churches being formed in all major towns and cities. To begin with, most believers came from the lower classes. There was much persecution, and many were put to death.

This persecution only came to an end when Constantine became Emperor, and from AD 313 Christianity was officially allowed, later becoming the state religion of the Empire. Now it was possible to worship freely and to preach the gospel. There were also problems.

Nominal professions of Christianity were made by those who only wanted to be seen in a favourable light, and to be employed in good positions in the state. Therefore it was important for the church to hammer out what it really believed. Great Councils were held to settle points of doctrine.

The first great divide among the churches came in 1054, although the differences went back some centuries. It was a split between East and West, each vying for authority. Greek Christianity, centred in Constantinople, led to the Eastern Orthodox churches. Latin Christianity, centred in Rome, became the Roman Catholic Church.

The next great divide was in the sixteenth century, the time of the Reformation, when there was a breakaway from Roman Catholicism under the leadership of Martin Luther. The Protestant churches came into being. They 'protested' against much Catholic teaching, especially the following, that:

(a) righteousness before God could be earned in any way: the Protestants said it could only be received as a gift through faith in Christ, crucified and risen;

(b) there was any other authority for belief alongside the
   Bible: the Protestants said that 'tradition' and the
   pronouncements of Councils etc. must be tested by
   the Bible;
(c) the Church should wield direct political power: the
   Protestants said it should not;
(d) a priest was necessary for access to God: the Protestants said that all true believers were priests, in the
   sense of having direct access to God through Christ;
(e) there are seven sacraments: the Protestants said that
   Jesus commanded only two, baptism and the Lord's
   Supper.

Since the Reformation, Christianity in some form has
spread to almost every country of the world.

Nobody knows exactly when Christianity first came to
Britain. It is possible it was through Christian Roman
soldiers being posted here. We do know that an officer in
the Roman army, Albanus, was put to death in 304 for
having sheltered a Christian priest. He is remembered as
St Alban, the first British martyr.

About 450, Patrick from England took Christianity to
Ireland. A little later, David was preaching in Wales, and
Columba from Ireland was in Scotland. By the time the
Pope sent Augustine to Britain in 597, Christianity was
already well established.

As a result of the Synod of Whitby in 664, Roman Christianity prevailed until the Reformation. During that turbu-
lent time, the Church of England came into being, striking
a middle way between the Roman Catholics and those, like
the Presbyterians, who wanted to be more radical and
biblical in their church life. The Presbyterians had to be
content with Scotland, and later Northern Ireland.

The Independents (later Congregationalists) would not
be put off by persecution from their radical understanding

of the Bible, saying that every individual church should be able to govern itself under God. The Baptists agreed, but insisted that baptism should be reserved for those who believed in Christ. An even more radical approach came with the Quakers, who accepted no authority at all except the Holy Spirit speaking to each believer. So the churches have multiplied, but it is important to notice that certain differences cut across the whole church scene. These are questions of church government, of authority for beliefs and of attitudes towards modern movements.

1 Systems of church government

Church government has developed along three main lines:

(1) *Episcopacy* (from the Greek word *episkopos*, literally 'overseer'). Here, there is what might be called, 'government from above'. Overseers, usually called bishops, are given considerable authority over the churches in a set area, a diocese. Important decisions affecting the whole Church are made by councils or synods, led by bishops, and must be implemented in the local churches, which are under their authority. It is usually said that bishops are the successors of the Apostles of the New Testament Church. Examples of this are the Roman Catholic Church, the Church of England and the Orthodox Church.

(2) *Presbyterianism* (from the Greek word *presbuteros*, 'elder'). Here, the elected elders of a local church have much authority over the life of that church. But a more important unit of government is the presbytery, made up of ministers and elders from each church in a district, and this exercises considerable supervision over those churches. The highest authority is the

annual General Assembly, whose decisions affect all churches. Examples of this, with various modifications, are the Church of Scotland, the Elim Pentecostal Church, the Methodist Church and the United Reformed Church.

(3) *Independency*. This denies that there should be any outside authority over the local church. Each church is competent to govern itself under God's direct leading. Most have government 'from below', with the church members, meeting together, having the final authority. Now an increasing number are governed by a body of elders. Examples of this are the Assemblies of God, the Baptist churches, the Congregational churches and those belonging to the Fellowship of Independent Evangelical Churches.

2   The final authority for belief

The question of *authority* is the most fundamental issue which cuts right across churches and denominations. How does God reveal truth to the church about what to believe? Where do standards come from? The answers to these questions determine the worship which takes place, what is preached, how the church is organised, and what the church expects of its members. Three different answers are given, and each of these viewpoints can be found in many denominations:

(i) *The Church*. Here, it is the official teaching of the Church which is accepted. It is believed that what the Church says, God says. The Bible is not enough by itself; it needs clarifying, and can be added to. The Holy Spirit has guided the Church in what it declares. This extra body of material is often called 'tradition'. Members must submit to the teaching of the Church.

This standpoint is found in the Roman Catholic Church, the Eastern Orthodox Church and the Catholic wing of the Anglican Church. For instance, in Roman Catholic understanding, the Church has been able to make authoritative statements about the infallibility of the Pope, the authority of the priest in the sacraments, and the importance of the Virgin Mary. The Bible and 'tradition' are both given authority. But it is the 'teaching office of the church' which alone can 'authentically interpret the Word of God'. (*Second Vatican Council*, 1962–65)

(ii) *Individual Reason.* Here, beliefs depend only on each person's reason or conscience. Truth is not objective, whether it comes from the Church or from the Bible. The Bible is helpful, and 'contains the word of God'. But it is a human document, and men make mistakes. There are inaccuracies in its history and its science. There must be a readiness to welcome new ideas, and if necessary, to discard traditional beliefs. We must respond to new discoveries and modern understanding. The essence of Christianity is life rather than particular beliefs. This position is often called Liberalism, and because it is subjective, not all believe the same things. Some suggest that God is not 'out there', but in the depths of one's own personality. It is usual to declare that miracles do not take place. The emphasis is more on changing society than on the conversion of individuals. Some would say that all religions lead to God. It is only in details that they differ, and all religions are valid. Most Liberals say that Jesus is not the eternal Son of God, but simply a good man who possessed the Holy Spirit to an exceptional degree. He made mistakes. Some say the death of Jesus was not necessary for God to forgive sins. His death was only a demonstration of supreme love. His resurrection was not physical, but spiritual, or only in the minds of his disciples. Some believe that God will eventually save all people, no matter what their lives or beliefs have been. Hell does not exist. For some, heaven does not, either. They deny 'the fall of man', and accept evolution. 'Situational ethics' are the key to living, not some objective code like the Ten Commandments. Every situation must be decided on personally at the time.

(iii) *The Bible*. Here, it is believed that the Bible contains all that is necessary for faith and life. It was written by people who were inspired by the Holy Spirit as he used their different personalities. It is the same Spirit who is given to recognise the Bible as the Word of God, who enables it to be understood, and its eternal principles to be applied to life. Other writings may help, but all teaching must be tested by the Bible.

This latter viewpoint is the position of **Evangelicals** (*evangelion* — Greek for good news, gospel). In recent years, they have become much stronger amongst the churches generally. They emphasise first of all the sinfulness of man, which leads to the judgment of God. The only hope of salvation and fellowship with God is through repentance towards God and faith in Christ, whose death, by bearing the punishment men's sins deserve, made acceptance with God possible. It is the Holy Spirit who 'convicts' and 'converts'. The terms 'Conservative Evangelical' and 'Liberal Evangelical' are still used to some extent. They describe two different groups of evangelicals. The 'Conservatives' are those who say that the Bible must be taken as it is, that God has not allowed errors to take place, even if the answer to some difficulties is not clear at the moment. Others, fewer in number, retain the teaching about the gospel and most features of evangelical life. They are not so sure about the reliability of Scripture in every detail, especially historically and scientifically. They subscribe to some aspects of critical scholarship.

'Fundamentalist' is a term used, often by opponents, to describe evangelicals who seem to be narrow and militant in their approach, who may be anti-intellectual, keep themselves separate and give the impression they have the whole truth.

Evangelical theology makes a difference between the 'universal' church, whose membership is known only to God, and is made up of all true believers everywhere, and the 'local' church, which may include on its membership roll those who are not true believers.

It is not surprising that, although there is agreement on the content of the gospel, there can be differences on secondary matters of biblical interpretation. One of these is baptism. Some favour infant baptism, others believers' baptism. The two different views are explained later under the Church of England (p. 50) and the Baptists (p. 24). Other differences are listed here.

a) The teaching about Creation

Though all believe that God is the Creator of the universe, some believe that his work of creation was confined to six literal days; others believe that the book of Genesis allows for the 'days' to be long geological ages, and that God used some sort of evolution.

b) The teaching about Election

In the New Testament, Christians are often referred to as 'the elect', or as being 'chosen'. The word 'predestined' is also used.

Reformed teaching, often called Calvinism after John Calvin (1509–64), defines the elect as those who have been chosen by God to belong to him. It is he who takes the initiative in their salvation by giving them the grace they need to repent and to have faith in Christ. Those he chooses will unfailingly and gladly come to him, and will be kept in that relationship by him for the rest of eternity. This latter is known theologically as 'final perseverance'. Christ died therefore only for the elect. All people are sinners and deserve judgment. But God, in his mercy and wisdom, has elected some for salvation. He uses mainly the preaching of the gospel to accomplish this. It is still the responsibility of those who hear to repent and believe.

'Hyper-Calvinists' so emphasize the sovereignty of God in salvation that they minimise the place of the human response. They do not engage much in evangelism, for they believe God will 'call' the elect with or without the preaching of the gospel.

Arminian teaching, after Jacobus Arminius (1560–1609), defines the elect as those whom God always knew would believe in Christ. God has given everybody enough grace to believe, if they choose to do so. It is up to them. Christ died for the sins of the whole world, so that God could forgive all who repent and believe. It is vitally necessary, therefore, to preach the gospel as widely as possible to give everybody a chance.

Because the emphasis is on human response, Arminianism teaches that someone who has been a believer can fall away, lose his faith and his salvation, and thus not go to heaven.

c) The teaching about Sanctification

This concerns the way Christians become more holy, more like Christ.

The Holiness movement ultimately stems from John Wesley in the eighteenth century. It teaches that there is a crisis experience, later than conversion, which can be enjoyed by those who earnestly seek it. This changes them inwardly in a dramatic way. Wesley called it 'entire sanctification' and 'perfect love', claiming that motivation towards sin could be eradicated from those who had this experience. But there must be intense spiritual effort to maintain and develop this new state of heart. A joyful love for God and others is now the overwhelming desire.

During the nineteenth century, the crisis experience became known as the 'second blessing'. A modification of Wesley's teaching was taught at the Keswick Convention. They denied that motivation towards sin could be eradicated. After the crisis experience, which comes through complete surrender to Christ, and is received by faith, the battle against sin is fought, not by striving oneself, but by passively trusting in the power of Christ. 'Let go and let God' became a well-known slogan. The Keswick Convention does not now stick rigidly to this teaching, but it is still widely held, particularly amongst those having an Arminian perspective.

Reformed teaching has declared that the new birth is such a decisive and dramatic experience that there is no need to look for a 'second blessing' for sanctification. The Holy Spirit is given when the new birth takes place, so that all the enabling is there to live a holy life. But the believer must not simply be passive. He must be obedient to what God calls him to be and to do, as set out in the Bible. He must wrestle with temptation, be patient and loving, always seeking to be more like Christ, whilst trusting in the power of the Holy Spirit to enable him. Sanctification is thus a gradual process. Perfection will not be attained in this life, although it is aimed for.

d) *The teaching about the Return of Christ*

All Evangelicals agree that Christ is going to return visibly and gloriously to usher in the end of the present world. At some point, there will then be a resurrection of the bodies of all who have died, and a final judgment day, when God will pronounce the eternal destiny of all, either to 'heaven' or to 'hell'. A new 'heaven and earth' will be created, where there will be no sin or suffering. Hell will be a place of punishment, but opinions differ as to whether the suffering will last for eternity or not. Some say it will. Others say it will finally lead to annihilation.

An important difference of opinion exists about the timing of the events, and the meaning of the Millennium, the period of 1000 years mentioned in Revelation 20:2–7. There are three main views:

(i)   *Premillennialism* — 'before the Millennium'. This says that when Christ returns, which could be at any time, there will be the resurrection of believers who have died. Then a literal reign of Christ will take place on the earth for 1000 years. Many Old Testament prophecies will be fulfilled during this time. The world will be a paradise, with a fruitful earth and even animals living together in peace. At the end of the Millennium will come the resurrection of unbelievers and the final judgment. The teaching has many variations of detail.

(ii) *Postmillennialism* — 'after the Millennium'. This says that before Christ returns, there will be a golden age, a period of prosperity and peace for the Church, not necessarily exactly 1000 years. The Holy Spirit will work in great power. There will be worldwide conversions to Christ, and he will reign spiritually on the earth.

(iii) *Amillennialism* — 'no Millennium'. This says that the 1000 years is not a literal period of time, but a symbolic term for the present era which runs from the resurrection of Christ until his return. He is now reigning spiritually.

Attitudes to modern movements

As well as differences between systems of church government and where authority for belief is centred, differences of attitude also exist among churches about the Ecumenical Movement and the Charismatic Movement.

The Ecumenical Movement

This has been the attempt to bring churches into a greater visible unity. Stimulated by the Edinburgh Missionary Conference of 1910, further conferences of church representatives were held to discuss differences in teaching and practice. The World Council of Churches was founded in 1948.

The World Council of Churches is a 'fellowship of churches which confess the Lord Jesus Christ as God and Saviour according to the Scriptures and therefore seek to fulfil their common calling to the glory of God, Father, Son and Holy Spirit'. Over 300 churches and denominations belong to it. Roman Catholics do not belong, but their official observers have played an increasingly significant role.

It has sought, not only to discuss, but also to implement programmes where churches work together, particularly in social action and education in the Third World. It also promotes schemes of unity between churches, locally and nationally.

In the UK, the Council of Churches in Britain and Ireland (CCBI) came into being as successor to the British Council of Churches. The Roman Catholic Church is a member of this. Under the auspices of CCBI, the Churches Together movement has been working at more local levels. Over twenty churches are members, with other organisations associated. They 'seek a deepening of their communion with Christ and with one another . . . to fulfil their mission to proclaim the Gospel by common witness and service in the world'.

Observations have been made that the theology used is often capable of more than one meaning, and is not based enough on the Bible. Also, it is observed that there is a variety of understanding as to what the gospel is, and therefore what a Christian is. It is claimed by some critics that the unity of the Spirit among true believers is more important than outward unity among churches.

The Charismatic Movement

This began in America in the late 1950s, and in Britain in the early 1960s. It introduced teaching which had been there in Pentecostal denominations, about the need for believers to have a 'baptism in the Spirit', and for the 'gifts of the Spirit' (e.g. those listed in 1 Corinthians 12:8–10) to be exercised in the Church. This teaching has spread through almost all denominations, and is often called 'charismatic renewal' or just 'renewal'. It has developed chiefly amongst those holding evangelical theology, but amongst many others as well, especially Roman Catholics. It hardly seems to have touched the Orthodox churches at all. It is said that something like half of all churches in the world are Pentecostal or charismatic, and in the UK, so are at least half of all evangelical churches.

The teaching: the 'baptism of the Spirit' is an experience which may take place either at conversion or afterwards, usually after intense seeking. It gives an assurance of being a child of God, as the love of God is experienced in a powerful way. This leads to a new effectiveness as a witness for Christ. As distinct from some Pentecostal teaching, the experience does not necessarily involve 'speaking with tongues', i.e. using a language in prayer which has not been learned, but is given by the Holy Spirit.

The 'gifts of the Spirit' (Greek *charismata*) are given to equip the Church in a supernatural way for its mission to the world, and include tongues, prophecies and healings. Churches are encouraged to actively seek God for these, at the same time 'testing' each one to see if it is truly from God. The movement has promoted a new freedom in worship, this often being lively and spontaneous, with congregational participation. Many new hymns and songs have become popular.

The teaching has its extremes and its variations. Most 'charismatics', for instance, strongly oppose **prosperity teaching**. This says that God means every Christian to be rich and to be perfectly healthy, and only a lack of faith prevents this happening.

The critics of the movement in general point out that looking for experiences can be dangerous, that these can be psychologically induced, and that one person's experience is not meant for everybody. There are those who say that the supernatural gifts of the Spirit were meant only for the time of the Apostles to authenticate their ministry, and died out when the Apostles died. Others would say that the gifts being seen today are not the same as those seen in New Testament times. There is the danger of having a thirst for the spectacular, with spiritual gifts not being tested sufficiently. They also point to the way individual churches have experienced splits because of the new teaching and ways of worship; and problems have occurred in some circles because of too strong an emphasis on the authority of leaders.

Those in the renewal movement say that this is **the way** the Holy Spirit is working today. It is similar to **New**

Testament times, and all churches should be seeking for this spiritual life and power.

The opposing positions are not as distinct as they used to be, and a growing respect for each other has been emerging, leading to greater co-operation.

PART 2

Afro-Caribbean or Black-led Churches

This covers a wide spectrum of groups and independent churches, mostly with a West Indian background, and mostly pentecostal. A few are linked to the African Independent Churches, and some have a 'holiness' emphasis. Most of the churches have arisen because of the great influx of immigrants since World War II, who found it difficult to integrate into the churches they attended here. In the 1950s the immigration rate increased rapidly. Most of those who came had had a Christian upbringing. But here they found the way of worship in traditional churches cold and formal, very different from that which they were used to. Also, British churches did not really give them a welcome, apart from pentecostal ones. So it was not long before they began to form their own churches, where they could find their identity and all would have a part to play.

Their progress has been quite remarkable. Now it is estimated there are over 200,000 adherents (far more than the membership) in over 3000 churches, nearly all in England. A large number of churches are independent or in very small groups. Many are associated with the African and Caribbean Evangelical Alliance or the Afro-Caribbean United Council of Churches.

The two largest denominations are the New Testament Church of God, over 7000 members in over 100 churches, and the Church of God of Prophecy, nearly 5000 members in 85 churches. Beliefs and organisation are similar. They have a centralised form of government and the final authority is in the General Assembly. National Overseers and District Overseers give more general leadership, with Pastors over the local church. Conferences and conventions are held regularly.

Their theology

It is possible to state this only in the most general terms. Their theology is usually strongly evangelical with belief in the Trinity and the need for new birth through faith in Christ. The pentecostal churches would say that speaking in tongues is the initial evidence of having been baptised in the Holy Spirit. Healing plays a major part, with, for example, the New Testament Church of God saying in their Declaration of Faith: 'Divine healing is provided for all in the atonement', i.e. that just as Christ paid for our sins at the cross, so he paid for our healing as well. They hold to the premillennial view of the return of Christ, that he will reign on earth for a period of a thousand years (p.14).

Holiness of living is expected, and it is often laid down what this involves, such as not to drink alcohol, smoke tobacco, or go to cinemas and dances. Some churches do not allow jewellery to be worn.

Many kinds of social projects are undertaken, e.g. homes for the elderly, nursery schools, respite care centres. In some places, they have organised a prison link work, with a 'return programme' helping to find jobs for those coming out of prison. They have a law centre, and counsel those who get into debt. A credit union is run.

Their church life

It has been said that their Christianity is not so much something to be understood as something to be experienced. This comes out in their worship services, which aim to stimulate the heart rather than the head. Worship is exuberant and can last quite a long time. Music and rhythm play a big part. They encourage creativity through the leading of the Spirit.

The pastor, often part-time, is given great respect, and the people look to him for leadership. At the same time, the congregation are expected to participate, women as well as men. The warmth of fellowship is something they rejoice in. The gifts of the Spirit are encouraged. Often all pray at the same time. Testimonies are frequently given to what God has done, e.g. in healing, for which there is regular prayer. Casting out of demons is practised.

Baptism is only for believers. Foot-washing may take place at Communion services.

Those churches linked to the African Independent Churches tend to have more ceremonial, more liturgy, and not to be quite so exuberant.

Many churches continue to grow, with evangelism an important priority. Some black observers feel that certain churches have become too respectable in recent years, and have veered away from their cultural heritage.

Most churches have a strong missionary interest, especially to African countries. Although in the past, these churches have not had much contact with other British churches, there is now a much greater desire by many leaders on both sides to build bridges.

Baptists

The first Baptist churches were formed in the early seventeenth century. Originally, there were two main streams: the **General Baptists**, whose theology was Arminian (p. 12), and the **Particular Baptists**, whose theology was Calvinistic (p. 11). They eventually merged in 1891.

The founder of the General Baptists was John Smyth (c. 1554–1612). He belonged to a 'Separatist' church (later to be known as Congregationalist). The Separatists had had to flee to Holland, because their beliefs about church government had led to persecution in England. Smyth, influenced to some extent by Mennonites and Anabaptists, came to believe that baptism in the New Testament was only for believers in Christ, and not for infants. (The Anabaptists, 'rebaptizers', were groups on the Continent at the time of the Reformation who also believed that true baptism was only for believers. But they were looked upon as subversive, and were persecuted because of some extremists and because they taught that the Church should be separated from state support and control.)

The first General Baptist church in England was formed in London in 1612 by members of Smyth's church, who had been able to return from Holland under the leadership of Thomas Helwys. The Particular Baptists (Particular because they believed that salvation was restricted to those elected by God) began in 1633 in London, when a Calvinistic Separatist church under Henry Jacob adopted believers' baptism.

By 1660 some 300 Baptist churches were in being. Persecution then came to all churches outside the Church of England, until the Toleration Act of 1689.

The eighteenth century saw General Baptists adopting unitarian beliefs, saying there was no Trinity, no deity of Christ. This led to a New Connexion being started in 1770. At the same time, the Particular Baptists became hyper-Calvinistic, the sovereignty of God so being stressed that there was no need for evangelism. It was men like Andrew Fuller who led the way to a renewal of life and evangelism. In 1785, Fuller wrote a book, *The Gospel Worthy of All Acceptation*, which had such an impact that the Baptist Missionary Society was formed in 1792. Their first missionary, William Carey, has often been called 'The father of modern missions'. Since then, Baptists have been in the forefront of Protestant missionary work. The BMS itself now works in many countries, especially India, Africa, West Indies and Brazil.

Baptists have always maintained that church and state should be separated, and were pioneers in pleading for freedom of conscience and religious liberty. One of their greatest preachers was C.H. Spurgeon (1834–92), who for 37 years preached to a congregation of 5000 in London, and through his inspiration, many new churches were founded.

It is probably true that the majority of Baptist churches today are descended from the 'Particulars', although their Calvinism is not always as explicit as it was at one time.

Their church government

Sometimes the phrase 'The Baptist Church' is heard, meaning all the churches together. This is technically wrong, because every Baptist church is independent. No outside body has authority over, or can speak for, the local church. The Baptist Union (see p. 27), for instance, can only advise. Inevitably, therefore, variations exist in belief and practice.

Each church elects its own pastor and church officers. Some churches have their pastor as the only elder, supported by deacons. In other churches, the pastor is one of a number of elders exercising spiritual leadership, with deacons having more practical responsibilities. In most churches, the leaders are accountable to the membership. 'Church meetings' are held at regular intervals, with the intention of being led by the Holy Spirit in the decisions made. Some churches give final authority to the elders.

Their church practice

The practice of believers' baptism is normally by complete immersion in water. Special baptistries are built for this purpose, often under the communion platform. Pouring water over the candidate (effusion) may be allowed, especially where health forbids immersion.

The practice of immersion is a portrayal outwardly of what happens when somebody becomes a Christian. Going down into the water represents death, the finishing of the old life; going under the water represents burial, the acknowledgement of death, that sins have been forgiven through the death of Christ; rising up out of the water represents resurrection, the new life that has been given, a life under the authority of the risen Christ.

Thus, for Baptists, baptism is only for those who are already Christians, not to make them believers. It is a 'confession of faith' in a public way, and should be undertaken as soon as possible after becoming a believer (most churches do not allow it before mid-teens). Some Baptist theologians say it is only a declaration of what has already happened; others say God does something deeper in the candidate. In any case, prayer is made for the Holy Spirit to come on those baptised, who will have given a testimony about God's work already in their lives, and perhaps answered questions about their faith.

Most Baptists believe that young children should not be baptised, because they cannot be believers in the New Testament sense. It is said that 'covenant theology' does not do justice to Scripture. Covenant theology states that, under the old covenant, infants born to the people of God (the Jews, descendants of Abraham) were circumcised; now, under the new covenant, baptism takes the place of circumcision, and children of the people of God (Christians) should be baptised.

The Baptist conviction is, that if there is a parallel between circumcision and baptism, baptism ought to be reserved for 'spiritual' children, those who have become believers through their preaching of the gospel. Under the new covenant, spiritual life cannot be inherited from human parents.

Most churches insist on baptism as necessary for membership. Baptist scholars endorse the view that, in the New Testament, baptism was the means by which believers came into membership. They became members through baptism. It was impossible to have one without the other. Today, this does not always follow. There are churches where membership comes later. Some allow baptism without membership.

Another school of thought is held by only a few. They accept those who believe they had a legitimate baptism as infants, but the church describes that baptism as only 'provisional'. It can only be described as baptism when it is completed by personal faith. Thus, these churches have 'open membership', accepting those baptised as believers or as infants.

Dedication services are held for infants, when a public thanksgiving is made for the child. The parents dedicate themselves to bring up their child in the ways of God (sometimes with church members agreeing publicly to help with this), and prayers are said for the child and family.

Worship services can vary greatly. Traditional worship can be found, with the minister leading, hymns being sung, the Bible being read, one or more prayers being made and a sermon being preached. But the charismatic movement (p. 16) has had a wide influence on Baptist churches. New 'spiritual songs' are sung in most churches, and many have congregational participation, perhaps with the gifts of the Spirit being exercised. On the other hand, some churches are definitely opposed to anything 'charismatic'.

Communion services are held regularly, some once or twice a month, others weekly, and are open to all who would call themselves believers.

Evangelism and missionary work have always been given a high priority. Baptists are found in all kinds of parachurch organisations, evangelistic and humanitarian; and overseas, not only in the Baptist Missionary Society, but in many interdenominational missionary societies. Most countries have Baptist churches, with the USA being especially strong. The Baptist World Alliance exists to promote fellowship, and has a programme of education, evangelism and social action. Worldwide membership is something over 67 million. In England: 163,000; Wales: 34,000, Scotland: 18,000, Ireland: 8000.

The Baptist Unions

In each of the home countries, most Baptist churches belong to their own Baptist Union. But some churches choose to be completely independent, or are members of the Strict Baptist denominations (see p. 30).

The Baptist Union of Great Britain

This is, in fact, for churches in England, and some English-speaking churches in Wales. Churches join voluntarily, but have to be accepted. An annual Assembly takes place, with representatives from the churches. Associations (26 in England, 3 in Wales) give fellowship and encouragement at a more local level.

Eleven General Superintendents give pastoral care to ministers, and generally advise churches. Through them, churches and ministers can be brought together when a new pastor is needed.

The BU has a list of accredited ministers (who can be men or women), but, except where a church is being financially helped by the BU, ministers do not have to be accredited for a church to appoint them. No official line is laid down generally about homosexuality, but all ministerial candidates have to comply with certain rules, one of which says, 'Homosexual genital practice is unacceptable in the Pastoral office'.

The BU itself is involved with the ecumenical movement, although many individual churches do not wish to have any connection with it.

Mainstream

Although Baptists had evangelical roots, liberal teaching
(p. 9) had a wide influence in the nineteenth century, as in
other denominations. This continued into the twentieth
century, and in the late 1970s, Mainstream was formed as
a rallying-point for evangelicals (p. 10), with the slogan,
'Baptists for life and growth; a Word and Spirit network'.

There is no formal membership, but with annual conferences, a regular newsletter and various activities, they
have seen an upsurge in evangelical life. Mainstream supporters have been appointed to certain senior positions in
the BU.

The main aim now is to bring about a national mission
strategy, with new churches being planted. A high proportion of those involved have been influenced by the
charismatic movement (p. 16).

BARB

In 1968, some who had a more liberal theology (p. 9)
formed what is now called 'The Broad Alliance of Radical
Baptists'. Through a newsletter, annual conference and
seminars at the BU Annual Assembly, they seek 'to encourage an awareness of the radical implications of the
Gospel of Jesus Christ', and 'to promote ecumenism, particularly amongst Baptists'. Their great concern is for liberty and tolerance, theologically and politically, and for
social issues like homosexuality.

The Baptist Union of Wales

Baptists have been numerous in Wales since John Myles
(1621–84) formed the first church at Ilston, near Swansea,
in 1649, and Vavasour Powell (1617–70) led a team of

itinerant evangelists. The first churches were Calvinistic in doctrine (p. 11), and suffered persecution after the Restoration in 1660. A Welsh Association was formed in 1700. Support was given by Baptists in England, especially by some leading Welsh-speaking ministers. Gradually, the churches became more distinctively Welsh, because of their own language and culture, with the chapel being the centre of a close-knit social life. One well-known preacher was Christmas Evans (1766–1838).

The Baptist Union of Wales was established in 1867. Churches who belong may use Welsh or English, and some use both. The Union, with its eleven Associations, has both Welsh and English Assemblies.

Another group of Welsh churches belongs to the Baptist Union of Great Britain.

The Baptist Union of Scotland

Although Baptist principles were first carried to Scotland via Cromwell's soldiers and chaplains in the mid-1600s, later the churches were greatly influenced by the teaching of Archibald McLean (1733–1812), whose conception of faith was simply an assent to the facts of the gospel. His followers were known as 'Scotch Baptists' or 'Sandemanian Baptists'. The movement under Robert and James Haldane also played its part, as did certain Baptists who came from England.

For a time, there were different streams running at the same time, and attempts were made to unite them. Finally, the Baptist Union of Scotland was formed in 1869. Now, a Superintendent gives oversight, and an annual Assembly takes place. The Union is not involved with ACTS, the Action of Churches Together in Scotland.

The churches are nearly all evangelical (p. 10), with some having a charismatic emphasis (p. 16). Women cannot be ministers. Usually, the pastor is the only elder, with deacons assisting him. Weekly Communion is quite common, and laymen can preside at the table.

Social work includes homes for the elderly and for the mentally handicapped, youth centres, hostels for homeless girls, and flats for alcoholics.

The Baptist Union of Ireland

In 1814, the Baptist Irish Society was formed by London ministers to assist in the work of evangelism in that country. A few Baptist churches had been founded, mainly through Army officers. Still, not much headway was made, and the famines of the 1840s, with many dying and others emigrating, led to some rethinking. It was decided to concentrate on the north, and in 1887, to transfer the leadership to Ireland itself.

Now there are 93 churches in the North, 16 in the South, in the Union. Pastors, elders and deacons are the church officers. They are wholeheartedly evangelical (p. 10). In the Doctrinal Statement, they declare 'the verbal inspiration and total inerrancy of the Holy Scriptures . . . as originally given by God; their sole sufficiency and final authority in all matters of faith and practice . . . the justification of the sinner by God's grace through faith alone in the Lord Jesus Christ'.

Many missionaries have been sent out from the churches.

Strict Baptist Churches

These are mostly in England, and there are two groups, the Grace Baptists and the Gospel Standard, arising originally from the Particular Baptists. Both are Reformed in their theology (p. 11), and are 'strict' in allowing only those to participate in the Communion service who have been baptised as believers. Some churches only allow those who belong to their own church or denomination.

Church government is independent. In the Gospel Standard churches, pastors are appointed by some, but visiting ministers go round on a regular basis. Grace Baptists are usually thought of as being more outward looking, more involved with evangelism and church co-operation. The Grace Baptist Mission works especially in South India, Africa, Europe and South America.

Membership: Grace Baptists over 10,000, Gospel Standard about 6000.

Chinese Churches

In 1948, Stephen Wang came to study in London before taking up an academic appointment he had been offered in the USA. In fact, he was so deeply moved by what he saw as the great need of the Chinese people in Britain and Europe that he decided to stay. He was particularly concerned for those working in restaurants. In 1951, he started the Chinese Church in London. He also founded the Chinese Overseas Christian Mission (COCM) to reach out into other cities in the UK, and then into Europe and the USA. He died in 1971, but a solid foundation had been laid. Now, in this country through the COCM, thriving churches are found in Birmingham and Manchester, with some smaller fellowships in other cities. Altogether, membership is over 5000.

Although the churches are mainly for the Chinese, especially for students, restaurant workers and professional people, other nationalities are also involved. They see themselves as interdenominational in character, and enjoy fellowship with other evangelical (p. 10) churches. Those who become members do not have to relinquish membership of a denomination or church to which they have previously belonged. But they must confess Christ as Lord and Saviour, be baptised, subscribe fully to the Statement of Faith, and have attended for six months.

Their beliefs

The Statement of Faith includes the following: 'The divine inspiration and entire trustworthiness of the Holy Scriptures as originally given and its supreme authority in all matters of faith and conduct. The redemption from the guilt, penalty and power of sin only through the sacrificial death (as our Representative and Substitute) of Jesus Christ, the Incarnate Son of God. The indwelling and work of the Holy Spirit in the believer and His sovereign action in bestowing spiritual gifts to God's people for the upbuilding of His church.'

Their church life

Baptism is for believers by immersion, and babies are dedicated. The Lord's Supper is held monthly, when any Christian believer can participate.

In London, there are in fact seven congregations which make up 'The Chinese Church in London'. Others are being planned. Each holds Sunday worship services. In the central congregation, a service is held in the Mandarin Chinese language, with interpretation into English; but other services are held in English and Cantonese. The other congregations use mostly Cantonese (the dialect spoken in Hong Kong). In the services, members of the congregation often participate, and spiritual gifts are exercised.

The overall responsibility is in the hands of the Church Council, which includes pastors, elders and one deacon from each congregation, as well as other church officers. Elders are nominated by the Council, and then recommended to the membership for approval. The final authority ultimately belongs to the members in a church meeting.

They see the spiritual work of the Church as most important, but much social work is also carried on, e.g. counselling, translation, and hospice visitation.

Christian Brethren

The man usually looked upon as the founder was John Nelson Darby (1800–82). He had been a High Anglican clergyman in Ireland, but from his reading of the Bible, he came to believe that not only was there a need for personal salvation and holiness of life, but that worship should be simple. Anybody could break bread with God's people, and Communion should be held every Sunday. Ordination was not necessary to preach the gospel. When Christians met together, the Lord would be amongst them, and minister to them. He also became convinced of the imminent return of Christ.

Others who were associated with Darby in the early days included A.N. Groves, who became a missionary to Baghdad and India, S.P. Tregelles, a New Testament scholar, and George Muller, whose homes for orphans in Bristol became well known. The first centres, round about 1830, were in Dublin, Plymouth and Bristol. There was such a strong group in Plymouth, with over a thousand members, that the movement became popularly known as 'Plymouth Brethren'.

They prospered because many left the Church of England, dissatisfied with its spiritual life, and having a desire for fellowship across the denominations. The Brethren have always rejected any form of 'clericalism', i.e. the authority of clergy, believing strongly in 'the priesthood of all believers'.

The early leaders believed the existing denominational structures were not sanctioned by the New Testament, often calling members of those denominations to separate from 'apostasy'. The Plymouth group felt they alone were the true church.

Darby travelled extensively, and when he died, he left behind, not only many volumes of his writings, but about 1500 churches in Britain, Europe, North America, Australia and New Zealand, each of which looked to him as their founder and guide. Now, most countries in the world have Brethren churches.

The two branches

In 1849, there came a split in the movement, into the **Open Brethren** and the **Exclusive (or Closed) Brethren**. B.V. Newton, the leader in Plymouth, was accused of heresy. Although he withdrew some of the statements he had made, Newton and Darby still did not agree about certain matters. Newton left the Plymouth assembly, but had the support of Bristol, whose leader was George Muller.

The split has never been healed. The main difference today is that whereas Open Brethren mix with other Christians, and may welcome them at the Lord's Table (Communion), the Exclusives keep to themselves, believing it is not right to mix at all, even socially, with those who are not 'in fellowship' with them. That includes Open Brethren. 'Household baptism' is practised, children of members being baptised when they are quite young. Open Brethren usually reserve baptism for believers only.

Exclusives are not very large in number, and there are different groups among them, e.g. the Reunited Brethren, which includes the former Glanton Brethren; the Tunbridge Wells Brethren; the Kelly Brethren; and the Plymouth Brethren, the largest Exclusives group, who follow the teaching of Raven and Taylor. They have often been criticised for being too authoritative and legalistic, although some groups are more so than others.

In contrast, Open Brethren churches are autonomous, each running their own affairs, and this has led to variations of practice. Many assemblies have now become Evangelical churches, often with some departure from traditional Brethren teaching and practice. But they would all see themselves as being conservative evangelical (p. 10), with perhaps one in ten having charismatic (p. 16) input, practising the gifts of tongues, prophecy and healing. Other groups say that these gifts are not meant for today. Although churches traditionally have not had paid pastors, now about one in five churches have some kind of full-time worker. They also support travelling Bible teachers and evangelists, as well as a great number of missionaries overseas.

The Brethren have always played a big part in evangelical inter-denominational activities, especially evangelism, but have had little to do with the ecumenical movement.

Numbers of all Brethren in the UK are in the region of 80,000, with over 60,000 Open Brethren, two-thirds of them in England.

Their worship

The Lord's Supper, or 'Breaking of Bread', has always been the central feature of worship. This is held every Sunday morning, when they trust the Holy Spirit to guide them in all they do. The meeting is open for anyone to take part by announcing a hymn, reading from the Bible or

bringing a message. Women have not usually been allowed to take part in prayer or speaking when men are
present, although some assemblies now allow this. Visitors may need a letter of introduction, or be commended
by a member, to take part in the Communion.

About two-thirds of churches also have a teaching
meeting, often later on a Sunday morning, when the Scriptures are taught systematically. Brethren have been known
for their knowledge of the Bible. The evening service is
nearly always evangelistic, preaching the gospel to those
who may not be Christians.

Their church government

Responsibility for the spiritual life of the church is in the
hands of elders, often called the oversight. New elders are
usually appointed by the present oversight, sometimes
after consultations with members. In a few churches, elders are elected by members. Any elder may take a baptismal service, a wedding or a funeral. About a third of
churches have deacons as well.

Conferences of church leaders are held from time to
time to consider Brethren principles and practice. It is rare
for women to be in leadership, and then only in smaller
churches.

Practice about membership varies. Some churches have
lists of those committed to membership, others are more
informal, with lists of those regularly attending who are
thought to be believers, and who are 'not known to be
tolerating serious sin'.

Interest in prophecy

Prophecy is of great interest among them, especially Premillennial (p. 14) teaching about the return of Christ.

Brethren used to be known for their teaching on **dispensationalism**, as put forward, for example, in the Scofield Bible notes. It is the belief that history can be split into time periods, dispensations, during each of which God has a special purpose, and people respond either with or without faith. From Adam to the millennium, there are at least six, including those of innocency (Adam before the fall), conscience (Adam to Noah), promise (Abraham to Moses), the law (Moses to Christ), grace (Pentecost to the rapture) and the millennium. There is now less support for this teaching.

Missionaries

A high proportion of Protestant missionaries overseas have a Brethren background. Some are sent out directly by assemblies; some (over 400) are linked to the Brethren support group, Echoes of Service; and some are with interdenominational missionary societies.

Churches of Christ

In the early nineteenth century, a movement began with the aim of 'the restoration of New Testament Christianity'. Its leaders were men like Thomas and Alexander Campbell in America and William Jones in England. Their background was Presbyterian. The outcome was the formation of the Churches of Christ in England, and the Disciples of Christ (sometimes known simply as the Christian Church) in America. Membership worldwide is somewhere between one and two million. A World Convention of Churches of Christ takes place every four years.

In 1980, about two-thirds of the churches in England and Wales joined the United Reformed Church. The rest formed 'The Fellowship of the Churches of Christ in Great Britain and Ireland', although a number of churches remained completely independent. Membership of the Fellowship is about 1000 in 35 churches.

Their Church order

Each church is independent, governed by their own elders and deacons. Some churches also have ministers, who are treated as fellow elders. They do not take the title 'Reverend' or wear clerical collars. No distinction is made between 'lay' and 'ordained'. The Fellowship has an annual Conference, but this has no authority over the individual churches.

Their beliefs

There is no Basis of Faith. They say that the New Testament is a sufficient guide for faith and order. They do not use the historic creeds, saying that they can easily become tests of fellowship. The only requirement for somebody to be baptized (and therefore to come into membership) is to affirm, 'I accept Jesus as the Christ, the Son of the living God.' For them, baptism is a necessary part of becoming a Christian. As well as repentance for sin and a confession of Christ, they teach that it is through baptism that there comes the assurance of sins being forgiven and the gift of the Holy Spirit. Baptism is necessary in order to be 'born of water and the Spirit'.

The Lord's Supper is held every Sunday, and this is the central act of worship. Anybody whom the church chooses may preside, but normally it is an elder, deacon or minister. Open prayer is always included, and anybody may be called upon to preach, read or pray. Communion is open to members of other denominations.

The London Church of Christ (or Birmingham, Manchester, etc., also called simply The Christian Church) is another movement which has arisen in recent years, with the same background, with similar doctrines, but with a very different method of working. They are completely separate from The Fellowship of Churches of Christ in Britain.

The London Church of Christ was started in 1982, and since then, others have been formed, e.g. in Birmingham and Manchester. They have their origin in the teaching of the Campbells in America, and in fact, the London Church of Christ was started by missionaries of the Boston (USA) Church of Christ. They are part of the International Church of Christ whose headquarters are in Hollywood, USA.

They accept the Bible as the only source of authority, and encourage both group and personal Bible study. But the impression is given that they are the only true Church. They criticise all other churches, especially condemning Reformed (p. 11) (Calvinistic) teaching on original sin and predestination.

There is agreement with the distinctive teaching of other Churches of Christ, that for salvation, not only is faith in Christ necessary, but baptism as well. It is also taught that salvation can be lost, if wholehearted commitment to Christ is not continued.

All members have to commit themselves to evangelism, which includes talking to people on the street. They have concentrated on reaching students, often by starting Bible study groups in college. Some universities have banned them from their campuses. Criticism has been made of the authoritarian demands they make on their members, continually putting pressure on them to be 'fruitful' in evangelism and to give money to the Church. The leadership must not be questioned. The Church denies putting pressure in this way, saying that whatever anybody does is voluntary, and pointing to their very large membership, attracted by the worship, Bible study and general friendliness.

The Church of England

The Church of England is only one part of the worldwide fellowship called the Anglican Communion. This is found in 164 countries, in 31 self-governing churches (groups of local fellowships), with a membership of about 53 million. Britain, Australia, Africa and North America are the main areas. The churches vary in their titles, e.g. 'The Episcopal Church of' (a church with bishops), or 'The Church of the Province of' or 'The Anglican Church of'. The Churches of Scotland, Ireland and Wales are also self-governing.

Thus, any measures which the Church of England passes, do not necessarily apply in other countries. Each church must decide for itself. Because of this, practices can vary in each 'Province'. The unifying factors are: that everywhere the Prayer Book is adhered to; baptism is practised in the Name of the Father, the Son and the Holy Spirit; and Holy Communion is central to worship.

Each church is also 'in communion' with the Archbishop of Canterbury. He presides at the Lambeth Conference, a gathering every ten years of the bishops of the whole Anglican Communion. The Anglican Consultative Council, made up of clergy and laity, meets every two or three years.

Some significant moments in their history

The Church of England came into being in the sixteenth century, a breakaway from the Roman Catholic Church in the reign of Henry VIII. The great architect of the new church was Thomas Cranmer (1489–1556), the Archbishop of Canterbury at the time. He agreed with the king in breaking away from Rome, but he also wanted a reformation in the Church. The reasons for this included:

(a) many of the bishops had more than one diocese and were rarely seen in them anyway;
(b) the monasteries had accumulated vast wealth;
(c) the morals of the clergy left much to be desired.

Cranmer was convinced of the authority of the Bible, and that salvation is only through faith in Christ.

Much was allowed to continue as before, e.g. the worship was to be liturgical, the organisation was to be based on the parish, the oversight was to be episcopal (by bishops), infants were to be baptised (paedobaptism), and the relation with the state was to be 'established'. Perhaps his greatest legacy to the Church was the first English Prayer Book, which he compiled. The modern Book of Common Prayer is substantially the same as his.

In the reign of Elizabeth I, the character of Anglicanism was worked out in much the same way as Cranmer had suggested. It has varied little since that time. Known as the Elizabethan Settlement, it is the *via media*, 'the middle way' between medieval Catholicism and the out and out reformation some people felt was necessary.

An important decision was taken in 1662, when the Act of Uniformity was passed by Parliament. This demanded the use of the Prayer Book in every kind of church service in the land. Two thousand ministers refused and were ejected from their 'livings'. Many set up their own independent chapels, the beginnings of Nonconformity.

The Methodist revival of the eighteenth century had a big impact because the main preachers of the revival, like the Wesleys and Whitefield, were members of the Church of England.

In the nineteenth century, great social reformers arose, men like William Wilberforce and the Earl of Shaftesbury. Also at that time, the Oxford Tractarian Movement, led by John Henry Newman and Edward Pusey, regained much ground for what has usually been called the High Church, or Anglo-Catholicism.

One of the most significant developments in worship came in 1980 with the publication of the Alternative Service Book. This has given rise to much more variety in church services, which some have welcomed and some have not.

The 'Established Church'

Henry VIII was declared 'supreme head of the Church of England', and since then, the British sovereign has to be a member of the Church. He or she is now called 'supreme governor', and in practice, exercises authority mainly through the prime minister. In this way, it is the 'established' church, the official Church in England (not in Scotland, Wales or Ireland). This means it is closely linked to the public life of the nation, and serves the country as a whole. Twenty-six senior bishops sit in the House of Lords. Archbishops, diocesan bishops and cathedral deans are officially appointed by the sovereign, although in practice, names are passed on from the Church through the prime minister.

The Church does not receive money from the state, but has income from property and investments, as well as from voluntary giving through the churches. The Church Commissioners use this income to pay clergy salaries and pensions, provide clergy homes, etc.

England is divided into two provinces, Canterbury and York, each with an Archbishop. That of Canterbury is senior, and he is the leader of the whole Church, although he does not have any real authority over other bishops. The provinces are divided into dioceses, at present 43 in number, each under the supervision of a bishop, who is helped by area bishops (sometimes called suffragan or assistant bishops), whom he chooses himself.

The principal church of a diocese is the cathedral, where the bishop has his 'throne' (in Latin, *cathedra*). Each diocese is divided into archdeaconries, these into rural deaneries, and these into parishes. Membership is about 1.3 million, although this simply means this number of names is on the Electoral Roll (not to be confused with the Local Authority Electoral Roll). The minimum requirement to be on the Roll (numbers revised annually) is to live in the parish, to have been baptized, and to be a member of the Church of England or a Church in communion with the Church of England. About a million people attend Sunday services in the 16,000 or so churches.

The parishes

The vicar (or rector, as he may be called for historical reasons) is responsible for the spiritual well-being of everyone who lives in his parish, whether Anglican or not. He has a right to call on anyone at any time, just as all parishioners have a right of access to the Parish Church, a right often claimed for marriages and funerals.

The vicar will have been ordained by a bishop. He often has a curate or deaconess to assist him, along with readers, lay men or women authorised to lead services and to preach. Women can be ordained and become vicars, although there is no legislation at present for them to become bishops.

Some vicars run more than one parish. In some urban situations, a team rector may head a group of churches each with its own vicar. Lay elders sometimes share the spiritual oversight.

Each parish has a Parochial Church Council, elected by those on the Electoral Roll, to help run the affairs of the parish. A Parochial Church Meeting is held at least once a year.

The chief lay officers of a parish are the churchwardens, elected annually. They are representatives of the bishop. Amongst other duties, they see that order is maintained inside and outside the church buildings, also playing an important part when a new vicar is to be appointed. The ultimate right to appoint a vicar belongs to the 'patron', who may be the Crown, the bishop, a society or an individual, depending on the history of the parish. But consultations are made first.

As well as catering for spiritual needs, and often having a counselling service, some parishes have a specialised ministry to the homeless and needy, those with AIDS, etc., perhaps by running a day centre or a night shelter.

The General Synod

Important decisions affecting the whole Church concerning doctrine, worship, finance, etc., are made by the General Synod. This meets at least twice a year. It comprises three 'Houses', of Bishops, of Clergy and of Laity, altogether over 570 members. All the Houses must have a majority for any measure to be passed. Dioceses and deaneries also have their own synod.

Although the General Synod has a vitally important role, the bishops themselves still have a traditional authority. In recent years, for instance, the question of homosexuality has been debated in the Church, and the bishops have given their ruling that lifelong homosexual relationships are allowed for lay members, but not for the clergy. This is seen as the policy of the Church.

The organisations

A vast number of organisations work within the Church, with a wide-ranging programme of spiritual and welfare work. Here are some of them:

(a) *The Church Army*: has about 400 evangelists. Most work in parishes alongside the clergy. Many are involved with planting new churches. They also provide homes for the elderly, hostels for the homeless, and give help to prisoners and their families, etc.

(b) *The Missions to Seamen*: has 180 missionaries in 100 ports at home and abroad.

(c) *The Church Pastoral Aid Society*: has workers helping in parishes and amongst young people generally. The Society publishes evangelistic and educational material.

(d) *The Children's Society*: aims to help any child in need. One of the largest adoption agencies in the country, they also employ social workers to help families, run day-care and residential homes, schools and nurseries for the handicapped and hostels for mothers and babies.

(e) *The Mothers' Union*: aim is 'to strengthen and preserve marriage and Christian family life'.

Missionary work overseas is carried out by a number of Anglican societies, the biggest of which is the Church Missionary Society. Amongst others are Crosslinks, the Intercontinental Church Society, the United Society for the Propagation of the Gospel, and the South American Missionary Society.

It is not always known that Anglican Monastic Communities are dotted about the country. Ten are for men only, thirty-eight for women only, and one is mixed. Almost all conduct retreats, some farm, many distribute food to the poor, some have theologians who do research and write. Fewer monks and nuns go into the communities now than used to be the case.

The form of worship

Since the Reformation, the way of worship has been laid down in the Book of Common Prayer, which is a unifying force in the Anglican world. When, in 1980, the Alternative Service Book was allowed to be used, it caused quite a stir. For one thing, it uses contemporary language which critics compare unfavourably with the literary quality of the Prayer Book. On the other hand, it is pointed out that it was not meant to be a substitution for the Prayer Book, only an alternative. It is now widely used.

Its introduction has meant that church services can vary greatly in style from one church to another — from simple to elaborate, from evangelical to catholic, from charismatic to traditional. Nevertheless, the main parts of the 'liturgy' will usually be included in some way. In the Parish Communion, often the main service of the day, the congregation will join in confession of sin, set prayers, singing hymns and psalms, repeating the Nicene Creed, hearing Bible readings and a sermon.

The two sacraments practised are baptism and Holy Communion, both of which must be led by an ordained minister of the Church of England. An adult may be baptised when he becomes a Christian, if he has not been baptised as a baby. More commonly, Infant Baptism takes place, and through this, babies are brought into the family of the church. They are seen as being included in God's covenant of grace with the parents. Just as Jewish babies were circumcised as a sign of their being in the covenant between God and his people in the Old Testament, so now, the teaching goes, babies are baptized as a sign of the New Covenant between God and his people. After the baptism, the priest says (in the words of the ASB 1980) 'We thank you that by your Holy Spirit these children have been born again into new life, adopted for your own, and received into the fellowship of your Church'.

Any parishioner has the right to have his child baptized. At the service, godparents make promises and affirmations of faith on behalf of the child, and are expected to help him with his faith as he grows up. At confirmation, which is taken by a bishop, the promises made by the godparents are now 'confirmed' in a personal way, and an open confession of discipleship is made. This leads to full membership in the Church. Well over half the confirmations take place at ages 10–13, and about a third between 14 and 17.

The Communion service, sometimes called the Eucharist or occasionally Mass, is usually considered to be at the heart of the church's life. In most churches, during the service, the people come to the front of the church, and kneel to receive bread and wine, symbols of the body and blood of Christ. Baptized members of other denominations may be allowed to participate.

Although most parishioners have the right to be married in their own parish church, the vicar can refuse if one of the partners has been divorced. He may allow another priest to take the service. The church is officially against remarriage after divorce, but it does take place. The whole matter is under discussion.

The teaching

The Anglican Church does not have a Confession or Basis of Faith as many churches do. A summary of teaching can be found in the Thirty-nine Articles of Religion, finally agreed in 1571. Their main purpose was to show how the Church differed from the Roman Catholic Church. Many of the statements are now interpreted in different ways, and the Articles generally have little influence. Now, instead of clergy having to give assent to the Articles, they need only 'affirm and declare their belief in the faith which is revealed in the Holy Scriptures and set forth in the catholic creeds, and to which the historic formularies of the Church of England bear witness'.

The Church has always aimed to hold together people who have different theologies. A bishop once said that trying to define the Church of England was rather like chasing a lightly poached egg on a piece of toast. Beliefs and practices vary considerably.

A common saying is that the Church is Catholic and Reformed. It is 'Catholic' in the sense that it has a continuity with the Church before the Reformation (and with most of Christendom today), with the essential features of Scripture, creeds, sacraments and ministry. This includes the three-fold ministry of deacons (who usually become priests after about a year), priests and bishops, all of whom have been ordained by bishops who are in the 'apostolic succession', i.e. tracing their ordination back through other bishops to the Apostles. The Church is 'Reformed' in that it does not have those features of the pre-Reformation Church which are considered contrary to Scripture.

Within that broad spectrum, these are some of the different hues: a considerable number of Anglicans see themselves as middle-of-the-road, with simply a loyalty to the Prayer Book and to the Church, enjoying the Parish Communion on Sundays, with its fairly short sermon, and not delving too much into theology. At the same time, three distinct theological groups can be seen, although some overlapping may occur.

Anglo-Catholics

These are sometimes called High Church, or the Catholic wing. They emphasise the historical continuity with Roman Catholic Christianity, e.g. episcopal succession, centrality of the Eucharist, and private confession to a priest. They have a 'high' understanding of the authority of the Church, i.e. the bishops and priests, and want to be as close as possible to Roman Catholicism, whilst remaining Anglican. The priest is seen as a mediator between God and his Church, and is called 'Father'. He wears eucharistic vestments.

Anglo-Catholics expect to receive the grace of God through the sacraments. A sung Eucharist is held on Sunday mornings, with a daily Eucharist or Mass during the week. Incense and votive candles are used, and a statue of the Virgin Mary may be in the church. They will often use 'the sign of the cross'. A 'Reserved Sacrament' will be in the church, i.e. when the Communion is finished, some bread and wine are kept in what is often called a 'tabernacle' to be on permanent display, to help with private prayer, and to give to those who are ill or dying. An 'Affirming Catholicism' group is not quite so strict as other Anglo-Catholics.

Some Anglo-Catholic churches have been influenced by the charismatic renewal. They believe in the liturgy, but make room for free prayer by the congregation and exercise of the gifts of the Spirit, including healing. Modern songs of praise are sung.

Since the late 1960s, the Anglo-Catholic Charismatic Renewal Group has been encouraging this through literature, Days of Renewal and conferences. Maintaining they have 'a rock solid reliance on the Scriptures, the word of God', they are sacramental at the same time. But just as 'Scripture that is not enlivened by the Holy Spirit is just words', so 'the Liturgy, when it is enlivened by the Holy Spirit becomes a powerful and power-filled medium for worship'. Sometimes, a 'Pentecostal Mass' is held.

Evangelicals

These are sometimes called Low Church, although the two have not always been identical. Since the 1960s, this branch of the Church has been growing in numbers and influence, and has some of the largest churches (p. 10). It is estimated that now about two-thirds of the clergy are evangelical.

Their main emphasis is on the authority of the Bible and the need to preach what it declares. 'Conservative Evangelicals' are convinced that it was God who caused the Bible to be written, and there is a unity about it, even an infallibility. But there are some, often called 'Liberal Evangelicals', who, although they accept the Bible's authority in general, also accept certain findings of critical scholarship, e.g. regarding the authorship of some books, and they question whether the Bible is always historically true.

Evangelicals generally preach (and sermons may be longer than the traditional C. of E. sermon!) about the seriousness of sin and the need to have faith in Christ for salvation, which leads to 'good works'. Salvation does not come through the sacraments, although these are important. The communion service is on Sunday mornings, and only rarely during the week. Some churches offer the dedication of infants as well as baptisms.

Lay people often help with the services. The only vestment the clergy wear is a surplice. Some wear a suit and tie, or even a pullover. It is common to address them by their first names.

Anglican Evangelical churches have been in the forefront of the charismatic renewal (p. 16), although some are opposed to it. It has been said that at least a quarter of the clergy have had some experience of it. 'The Anglican Renewal Ministries' aim to encourage the renewal through an annual conference for 400 clergy, and through literature and training courses. They point out that, although there have been casualties, churches and individual lives have been transformed, and a large proportion of ordinands (those training for the ministry) come from 'charismatic' churches.

'Reform' see themselves as a ginger group fighting for traditional Anglican doctrine (with the aim of evangelising the nation), and the media see them as the voice of Anglican evangelicalism, even though there are other groups, such as the Anglican Evangelical Assembly with its standing committee, the Church of England Evangelical Council. Reform has both charismatic and non-charismatic members. It has become known for its opposition to the ordination both of women and of practising homosexuals (the latter is not legal in the Anglican Church). At the same time, there are many evangelicals who welcome the ordination of women.

Reform leaders also maintain that bishops have not been definite enough in saying that sexual relations outside marriage are not right before God. They believe there is a need 'radically to reform the present shape of episcopacy and pastoral discipline, to enable local churches to evangelise more effectively'. Bishops should be mainly advisors and enablers.

Liberals

These are sometimes called radicals, and also Broad Church. They are concerned not simply to accept traditional teaching, but to carve out a theology which people today will accept (p. 9). So it is necessary to keep on exploring new theology and new practices. Everybody cannot possibly think in the same way about God and all need to work things out for themselves.

This approach leads to a wide variety of beliefs. Some common features are: the creeds are treated with reservation; Jesus is not looked upon as God, only as a good man; the interpretation of the resurrection is 'only that life with God is not broken by death'; miracles do not actually take place, but have symbolic meanings in the Bible; human beings are basically good, and evolution is a fundamental aspect of belief.

'The Modern Churchpeople's Union' encourages the 'search for truth by interpreting traditional doctrine in the light of present day understanding'. Through literature and conferences, views are exchanged on theological, political and social issues.

Facing the future

In the 1980s, the Anglican Church declined in numbers by about 15%, but in the 1990s the decline has been less. In fact, the number of new churches opening now exceeds the number of closures. Although many churches are struggling, others are increasing in numbers, especially those which are evangelical and charismatic.

The question of women priests is still an issue. Since 1992, when the measure to ordain women was passed by the General Synod, some 300 priests have left the Church because of it. Many joined the Roman Catholic Church or the Orthodox Church, although some have returned. Some formed a new church, the Anglican Catholic Church, to maintain Anglo-Catholic principles. Within the Church itself, 'Forward in Faith' is an umbrella movement for those opposed to women's ordination, mostly amongst the Anglo-Catholics, and 'Reform' speaks for evangelicals who are opposed.

'Flying bishops' have been appointed by the Church to try to help. In a diocese where all bishops are in favour of women priests, these 'Provincial Episcopal Visitors' as they are strictly called, are able to minister in parishes which are opposed, with the permission of the bishop of the diocese.

Another continuing source of debate is whether known practising homosexuals should be ordained. It has been said that the Church could be split even more on this issue than on the ordination of women, with even greater numbers leaving the church.

Question marks still hang over the 'establishment' of the Church, and the pros and cons are continually being discussed.

Anglican churches in the rest of the United Kingdom

These churches have similar teaching, services and organisation to the Church of England. The differences are minor.

The Church in Wales

Breaking away from the Roman Catholic Church at the same time as the Church of England in the sixteenth century, they were 'disestablished' in 1920. At that time, the Archbishop of Canterbury released the Welsh bishops from direct allegiance to himself, and he enthroned the Bishop of Asaph as first Archbishop of the independent Church of Wales. The Church has six dioceses, with about 87,000 members and is a member of CYTUN, Churches Together in Wales. Final decisions are made by the Governing Body, which meets at least twice a year. It is made up of the order of the bishops, the order of the clerics and the order of the laity.

Women are now allowed to be ordained as priests. A 'flying bishop' has been appointed to minister to those opposed to the measure.

The clergy are now allowed to remarry divorcees.

The Scottish Episcopal Church

At the beginning of the sixteenth century, religious life in Scotland was in a state of decay. However, through the Reformation and John Knox, new life appeared, beginning about 1560. The Reformed Church of Scotland was Anglican until 1689, when King William III declared it to be Presbyterian. From 1712, those who had remained faithful to episcopacy were allowed to worship separately from the Church of Scotland, as long as they used the English Prayer Book. But their support of the Jacobite cause, which was defeated in the 'Risings' of 1715 and 1745, led to their being outlawed, and they almost died out. At the end of that century, they were allowed again, and grew steadily during the nineteenth century.

There are now about 50,000 members. Widely used today is the Scottish Liturgy of 1982, although the 1929 Scottish Prayer Book, and the revision of 1970 are also used. The Church is a member of ACTS, Action of Churches Together in Scotland.

The bishops elect one of their number to be Primus (rather than Archbishop), who is 'first among equals'. Each of the seven dioceses has its own synod. The General Synod, meeting annually, is responsible for decisions affecting the whole Province. Ordination of women priests is permitted, but no 'flying bishop' has been appointed.

Divorcees may apply to their bishop to be remarried in church. The parish priest and the bishop make a judgment about each case.

As in the Church of England, there are Catholic, Evangelical and Liberal wings to the Church.

The charismatic renewal (p. 16) has not had the same impact in Scotland as in England, although possibly more in the Episcopal Church than in other denominations. The Scottish Episcopal Renewal Fellowship gives fellowship to those churches involved with the renewal, where there is usually lively praise, a healing ministry, and participation by members. Conferences and retreats are held by the SERF.

The Church of Ireland

In the 16th century, during the time of the Reformation, changes only took place in Ireland where the English monarch was acknowledged. Elsewhere, the Reformation was resisted as further English aggression. Over the centuries, the 'Protestant ascendancy', which arose through political power and land ownership, was increasingly resented. This led to the disestablishment of the Church of Ireland in 1869, and its independence.

The Headquarters is in Dublin. The Archbishop of Armagh is the Primate of All Ireland (elected by the bishops of the twelve dioceses), and the Archbishop of Dublin is the Primate of Ireland. The General Synod is the supreme legislative authority, consisting of the House of Bishops and the House of Representatives (which includes clergy and laity). Women can be ordained as priests. In Northern Ireland, membership is about 160,000.

In addition to the Book of Common Prayer, their own Alternative Prayer Book (1984) is used.

They declare themselves Protestant and Catholic — Catholic because they possess 'a continuous tradition of faith and practice, based on the Scriptures and early traditions, enshrined in the Catholic Creeds, together with the sacraments and apostolic ministry'; and Protestant (or Reformed) because they affirm their 'constant witness against all those innovations in doctrine and worship, whereby the Primitive Faith hath been from time to time defaced or overlaid'.

Church of the Nazarene

The name comes from Matthew 2:23, where Jesus is called a Nazarene; and also from Acts 24:5, where the early church was described as 'the Nazarene sect'. Although, in the nineteenth century, a small denomination in the USA was called 'The Church of the Nazarene', the Church as it is today is the result of a series of unions. Eleven small denominations, three of them British, all with a Wesleyan background, merged at different times between 1896 and 1958. One of these unions, in 1908, is taken as the official beginning of the Church.

Wesleyan holiness

Convinced evangelicals (p. 16) and Arminian (p. 12) in theology, they believe they were raised up to emphasise John Wesley's holiness teaching (p. 12). 'We believe that entire sanctification is that act of God, subsequent to regeneration, by which believers are made free from original sin, or depravity, and brought into a state of entire devotion to God, and the holy obedience of love made perfect. It is wrought by the baptism with the Holy Spirit, and comprehends in one experience the cleansing of the heart from sin and the abiding indwelling of the presence of the

Holy Spirit, empowering the believer for life and service'. It 'is wrought instantaneously by faith, preceded by entire consecration'.

The churches

Local churches have pastors. The two Districts North, including Scotland and Northern Ireland, and South, each have a Superintendent. The final authority for belief and practice is the General Assembly, held every four years. In the UK, there are nearly 100 churches, with something over 5000 members.

Baptism is for believers, and it may be by sprinkling, pouring or immersion. But 'young children may be baptized, upon request of parents or guardians, who shall give assurance for them of necessary Christian training'.

On the whole, worship services lean towards a traditional pattern, with the pastor leading, praying and preaching. But more congregational participation is coming in. Prayer for healing is encouraged.

The highest moral standards are expected, and these are spelt out. For instance, members must avoid entertainment and literature which might undermine morals. They must avoid alcohol, drugs and tobacco. Abortion is wrong, except for sound medical reasons, and homosexual acts are sinful before God. Tithing is encouraged, and they are strongly committed to evangelism and to missionary work overseas.

Congregationalism

Towards the end of the sixteenth century, there were Christians, led by Robert Browne (c. 1550–1633), who came to believe, from studying the Bible, that the local church should consist only of those who were true believers. They used the phrase 'the gathered church', and believed that each church could govern itself under the direct rule of Christ, without being under any outside authority. Their basic theology was Calvinistic (p. 11). Although Martin Luther had taught the 'priesthood of all believers', he did not put into practice what these people thought was the doctrine's logical conclusion.

They were Puritans who could not accept episcopacy or Presbyterianism (p. 7) as being the biblical idea of church government, coming to this conclusion: 'Each church has the right to elect its own officers, manage its own affairs, and to stand irresponsible to all authority, saving that of the supreme and divine Head of the Church, the Lord Jesus Christ'.

The Independents

To begin with, they were called Separatists or Independents, even Brownists. Many were persecuted for their beliefs, some being put to death. Elizabethan England had no room for those who did not agree with the Church of England. In exile in Holland, Browne wrote a pamphlet, *Reformation Without Tarrying for Any*. This was circulated widely and became very influential.

To seek freedom for their views, the Pilgrim Fathers (1620) were amongst those who went to North America. This ultimately led to churches with a congregational form of government becoming widespread across there (including Baptists).

Eventually, they were allowed in Britain. Independents formed the backbone of Oliver Cromwell's army. John Owen, one of the greatest of Puritan theologians, became Vice-Chancellor of Oxford University in Cromwell's time. In 1658, the beliefs of the Independents were expressed in the Savoy Declaration. In many respects it was similar to the 1642 Westminster Confession. In the eighteenth century, two well-known hymn writers, Isaac Watts and Philip Doddridge, were Independents.

Congregationalists were prominent in the founding of the London Missionary Society in 1795 (now Council for World Mission). The Congregational Union of England and Wales was formed in 1831. Today the International Congregational Fellowship links churches in different countries.

Continuing Congregationalism in England and Wales

In 1972, about four-fifths of Congregational churches in England and Wales (apart from the Welsh-speaking ones) joined with the English Presbyterian Church to form the United Reformed Church, which has a more centralised form of government. But there were those who wanted to keep to the original principles of Congregationalism. They are usually linked either with the

Congregational Federation or the Evangelical Fellowship of Congregational Churches.

The Congregational Federation

Formed in 1972, it does not have any legislative authority over the member churches, simply offering recommendations. Assemblies are held, usually twice annually. Area Assemblies also offer support and fellowship. It has no doctrinal basis, and therefore there is a diversity of theology. Over 300 churches belong to the Federation, with 12,000 members. They are committed to the Ecumenical movement, being members of Churches Together in England (p. 15).

The Evangelical Fellowship of Congregational Churches

Formed in 1967, there are now over 130 churches in the Fellowship, with 6000 members. They have a statement of scriptural principles drawn up as a 'Basis of Fellowship', but believe that 'each local church is in itself a complete church . . . possessing all the rights and responsibilities of the Church by the Holy Spirit — and is answerable only to Jesus Christ, and not to any association, conference, council, synod or any other ecclesiastical body'. Fellowship and counsel is encouraged with evangelical churches in other denominations or of no denomination but, unlike the Federation, they are not committed ecumenically. Some churches are 'charismatic' (p. 16) in their worship and life. All pastors are male.

The rest of the UK

Wales, Scotland and Ireland have their separate organisations: Wales (The Union of Welsh Independents for Welsh speakers) has about 42,000 members in nearly 600 churches; Scotland (Scottish Congregational Church) over 9000 members in 64 churches; Ireland (Congregational Union of Ireland) nearly 2000 members in 26 churches, mostly in Northern Ireland.

In Scotland, two main streams, one associated with the Haldane brothers and the other with James Morison finally merged in 1896 to form the Congregational Union of Scotland. Then in 1988, a proposal to unite with the United Reformed Church just failed to get the required majority. A process of reform took place leading to the formation of the Scottish Congregational Church in 1994. Many churches disagreed with the reforms, resigned, and are now associated with the Congregational Federation of England and Wales.

Although the meeting for members in a local church is still the ultimate authority for decisions affecting its internal affairs, there is now more of a presbyterian system in the Church. Representatives from each church make up Area Councils with responsibility for pastoral, missions and educational activities. Ministers are appointed with the agreement of the Area Council. An Assembly of the Church takes place annually.

A wide spectrum of theological positions is found in the Church, with the mainstream being liberal evangelical (p. 10). They play a leading role in ecumenical affairs in Scotland, and are much involved with the Council for World Mission.

In Ireland, Congregationalism was introduced in the seventeenth century through Oliver Cromwell's army, most of whose chaplains and soldiers were Independents. It is said that 150 ministers came to Ireland with Cromwell, including John Owen, the Puritan theologian, who became a Trustee of Trinity College, Dublin. The hymn writer, Thomas Kelly (1769–1855), erected chapels in a number of places.

English Congregationalists founded the Irish Evangelical Society in 1814. But it was not long before the Irish felt it was being led too much by English people, and a Congregational Union was formed in 1829. The early Congregationalists had been Calvinists (p. 11), but in the nineteenth century, liberal theology (p. 9) had a big influence. During most of the twentieth century, numbers decreased very considerably. Churches had to be closed.

In recent years, an evangelical (p. 10) emphasis has prevailed. In 1992 a new constitution was adopted, with an evangelical Doctrinal Basis. As well as having ministers, there is a Register of Pastor Evangelists.

The Union has nothing to do with ecumenical activity, but is a member of the British Evangelical Council, also having links with the Evangelical Fellowship of Congregational Churches in England and Wales.

The Authorised Version of the Bible (KJV) is used in church services, and ladies are expected to wear head coverings.

Congregationalist church practice

Congregational churches and Baptist churches are similar in many ways, except for baptism. Congregational churches usually practise infant baptism, although believers' baptism may also take place in some churches. Evangelical churches only baptize infants of believing parents.

The basic independence of the local church is maintained. This means that the theology held and preached varies quite greatly. The church meeting of members has the final authority for policy, as they seek to be led by the Holy Spirit. The members elect a pastor, and also deacons to help with the running of the church. Sometimes elders are also appointed. To become a member, it is enough in some churches to have the pastor's recommendation. But in most churches, recommendations have also to be made by others to the church meeting, perhaps by two members who have interviewed the applicant. Sometimes, a testimony must be given to the church.

Every member is expected to play a part in the life of the church. There is no set form of worship service, and they vary considerably. In most churches, a lay person, man or woman, is allowed to lead and preach at the Communion service, which may be once or twice a month.

Countess of Huntingdon's Connexion

Selina, Countess of Huntingdon (1707–91), was one of the outstanding figures of the eighteenth century, and especially of the Methodist Revival. As an aristocrat, she was accepted in the highest circles of the land, even in court circles, and did her best to see that the gospel was preached there. She was also known as the friend of the poor.

Living a simple life herself, she used her wealth not only to encourage those who preached the evangelical gospel, but to build chapels and to help people in need. She supported many chaplains, who ministered at the chapels she built. She supported George Whitefield, one of the great evangelists of the Revival.

The Countess had wanted to remain in the Church of England, but eventually she was forced out with her chaplains and chapels. In 1781, the Countess of Huntingdon's Connexion was formed, in which she had almost sole authority. Through her, 200 chapels and mission stations were opened.

The Connexion today

Since then, most of the chapels have either been closed or been absorbed into other denominations. Now, the

Connexion has about 25 chapels with some 1000 members. There is an evangelical Statement of Faith with a Reformed emphasis (p. 11). Some churches have been influenced by the renewal movement (p. 16), and have a free form of worship. Others are more traditional.

The Connexion basically favours infant baptism, but if a minister prefers not to administer this, he does not have to, but must allow another minister to do so.

The Trustees of the Connexion have responsibility for the chapels, and for appointing ministers. The churches are usually known as 'Evangelical Free Church' or 'Free Church'. Some have links with other local churches. Others keep themselves separate.

The Countess was strongly missionary-minded, and enabled many missionaries to go abroad. One country, Sierra Leone, has still a denomination called 'The Countess of Huntingdon's Connexion', with 18 churches. The Connexion in the UK helps to support them.

Free Church of England or Reformed Episcopal Church

The Church was started in 1844 by evangelical (p. 10) clergy in the West Country, who believed the Church of England was moving too far towards Roman Catholic beliefs and practices, as a result of the Oxford (or Tractarian) Movement. In 1927, they joined with the Reformed Episcopal Church of America. They see themselves as a Protestant Episcopal Church (p. 7), adopting outside the Church of England that which evangelicals hold within it.

They fully support the Thirty-nine Articles of Religion, which the Church of England accepted in the reign of Queen Elizabeth I mainly to show where they differed from the Roman Catholic Church. It is Calvinistic (p. 11) in tone.

The worship is liturgical, following a revised form of the 1662 Book of Common Prayer. The Lord's Supper is seen as a memorial, and not a sacrificial repetition. It is open to all believers. Infant baptism is practised, and confirmation is a public declaration of faith by those who are 'born again'.

The Church has a southern and a northern diocese, each with a bishop. Both dioceses have Synods twice a year. The annual Convocation makes decisions affecting the Church as a whole. At the local level, churches are led by 'presbyters' (not 'priests'). The laity are given a prominent role. The Church tries to make sure that they are not in competition with any evangelical church in the locality.

A strong missionary interest is maintained. In the UK, membership is 1500 in 25 churches.

Free Methodist Church

The Free Methodist Church was founded in the USA in 1860, and in the UK in 1960. They called themselves 'Free' because they spoke out against slavery and also against class distinction, which was seen then in churches who rented out pews to the wealthy. Now there was a Church where all seating was free!

The UK Church has strong links with the American organisation, coming under its umbrella. An American Bishop has overall pastoral responsibility for the UK as part of his area. But a British Superintendent has the day-to-day care of the churches, which are mostly in Lancashire and in Northern Ireland.

Local churches are led by pastors, who are appointed by a central committee after consultation with the church. Churches are autonomous to a high degree, but are ultimately responsible to the British or Northern Ireland Annual Conferences as well as the doctrines and rules of Free Methodism. These are evangelical (p. 10) and Arminian (p. 12), mostly following Wesley's teaching.

In the UK, they practise only believers' baptism. Members promise to abstain from alcohol, drugs and tobacco. UK membership is something over 1000 in 22 churches, although attendance figures are much higher. Throughout the world, the Church has Conferences in about 30 countries with much missionary activity.

Independent Churches

Throughout Britain, there are many churches which have either left a mainline denomination, or have not felt able to commit themselves to one, because of policies or theology of which they could not approve. Nearly all are evangelical in theology, and most have fellowship with other evangelical churches in the same area. Most are not involved with the ecumenical movement, because they believe it tolerates theological views which are not true to the gospel. It is estimated there are two or three thousand of such churches. Many are completely independent, but below are some of the ways they associate together.

The FIEC

In 1922, the Fellowship of Independent Evangelical Churches was formed, largely through the vision of E.J. Poole-Connor, to try to link these churches together. Now, some 430 belong, with about 34,000 members, and are usually entitled 'Evangelical Free Church'.

The FIEC gives advice on pastoral issues and church trusts, and alerts churches to significant issues affecting theology and ethics. It also supports its own evangelists and church-planters.

Each church is still self-governing, and they vary greatly. Some have a congregational form of government; with others, the authority is in the hands of elders. Over three-quarters have pastors, who belong to an accredited list. Some churches practise only believers' baptism; some have infant baptism. Some would be termed 'charismatic' (p. 16), others would be opposed to that emphasis. Reformed (Calvinistic) theology (p. 11) is usual. The all-important proviso is that each church subscribes to an evangelical Basis of Faith.

The FIEC Basis of Faith includes:

About the Bible: 'Every word was inspired by God through human authors, so that the Bible as originally given is in its entirety the Word of God, without error, and fully reliable in fact and doctrine. The Bible alone speaks with final authority, and is always sufficient for all matters of belief and practice.'

About salvation: 'Salvation is entirely a work of God's grace, and cannot be earned or deserved. It has been accomplished by the Lord Jesus Christ and is offered to all in the gospel. God in his love forgives sinners whom he calls, granting them repentance and faith.'

For fellowship, guidance and encouragement, they meet together at local level, and have an Annual Assembly at national level. A Council of Management is elected by the member churches. Regional 'Visitors' are chosen to advise churches and pastors, and to encourage co-operation and church planting.

Town and City missions

In the nineteenth century, town and city missions began to mushroom. The first was in Glasgow in 1826, started by

David Nasmith. Later, he started some 50 other missions, including the London City Mission, which now has about 100 missionaries. The movement spread to most towns and cities.

To begin with, their aim was to concentrate on evangelism, and then to link converts to the mainline churches. Mission halls, door-to-door visitation and open-air evangelism were some of the methods used. Nearly forty still continue in this way, but now also run medical clinics, day nurseries, and homes for the elderly. Work amongst the homeless, visiting hospitals and prisons are regular features of their work. In more recent years, most of the missions have become churches in their own right, often linked to the FIEC.

The Union of Evangelical Churches

This is separate from the FIEC, but they have an association together 'in the proclamation of the gospel and the defence of evangelical truth'. The churches are to a large extent independent, but are under the supervision of a central Council, made up of ministers. About 20 churches are involved, mostly in Essex, with some 600 members. They practise believer's baptism, and publicly pray for healing.

Associating Evangelical Churches in Wales

Over fifty independent evangelical churches in Wales have formed the AECW, for fellowship and church planting.

Independent Methodists

Peter Phillips is usually regarded as the founding father of Independent Methodism. He was the leader when four Methodist local (lay) preachers left the Methodist Society in Warrington in 1796, because they were told their cottage meetings must stop, and they were not prepared to comply. A new society was formed, which is still there today. A number of other churches (societies) began quite spontaneously, which had the same outlook as the Warrington church.

For many years, the only tangible link between them was an annual meeting and an exchange of preachers. Peter Phillips travelled widely as a preacher for over fifty years. Through him and others, many other churches were affiliated.

A variety of names was used by these churches. But in 1898, they decided to keep to one name, the Independent Methodist Connexion. In the UK, membership is now about 2500 in over 100 churches, mostly in the North of England. The Headquarters is in Wigan.

Their church life

Each church is autonomous, the members' meeting having the final authority for the way the church is run. Each church has its own system of membership and forms its own rules, although the Connexion gives advice. Churches are linked in circuits for fellowship and mutual help. The Connexion has its Annual Meeting, with delegates representing the churches.

Churches may call ministers, but they are not paid (although evangelists and missionaries are given financial support). Ministers train part-time for four years before being recognised as ministers by the Connexion. They have no exclusive functions in the churches, but do some preaching and pastoral work. Churches without a minister are led by a president or by elders. The churches have sent many missionaries overseas.

The Statement of Faith is evangelical (p. 10) and Arminian (p. 12): 'Salvation is God's purpose for all mankind and is only possible through personal faith in the atoning work of the Lord Jesus Christ.'

The doctrine of the priesthood of all believers is emphasised, that 'each believer has direct access to God through the Lord Jesus Christ'. Believers' baptism is practised, and the Lord's Supper observed regularly.

Jesus Fellowship Church

Originally, this was a Baptist church in the village of Bugbrooke, just west of Northampton. Noel Stanton became the pastor in 1957, and is still the overall leader. After a charismatic experience in 1969, he led the Church into experiencing the supernatural gifts of the Spirit, and they grew in numbers quite dramatically. Since then, the Church has developed along lines which they see as radical New Testament Christianity, with free charismatic worship, strict holiness of living, caring for one another and reaching out with the gospel in a variety of ways.

Perhaps their most distinctive emphasis has been on community. Over a third of members (which number about 2600 in different centres) live in community houses. These have somewhere between 6 and 60 people, who live together as a family. Those who are church members have a 'common purse', and share possessions. The houses act as the 'training and service' centres of the church.

They have also branched out into various business ventures, e.g. farms, health food shops, garages, road haulage. Everybody who works in these businesses is paid the same.

The evangelism is helped by both the community houses and the businesses. In 1987, the **Jesus Army** was set up, to mobilise outreach in towns and cities in the

Midlands, and then in London. They have targeted homeless young people, those involved with drug or alcohol
abuse and others in social need. Long-term care has been
given by integrating them into the houses, and into the
farms or other businesses. Their work in this way has
become well known, as has their campaigning against
crime, unemployment, homelessness, racism, abortion
and the occult.

Criticism has also come. In the mid-1980s, they were
asked to leave the Evangelical Alliance and the Baptist
Union because it was said they were isolationist, and had
poor relationships with other churches. In recent years,
they have sought to improve those relationships.

They have also been criticised for being too authoritarian and legalistic, laying down rules too strictly. Their
answer is that all they do is to encourage a simple lifestyle,
that 'as God's covenant people they are called to be separated from the spirit of the world'. Participation is voluntary, each person must decide for themselves, and they can
leave at any time.

They describe themselves as 'reformed, evangelical
(p. 10) and charismatic (p. 16), practising believer's baptism'. They uphold the Apostles' Creed, the Nicene Creed
and the Athanasian Creed. The leadership and authority
is in the hands of elders, who are always male. They
believe that every church member should be involved in
some way. Each one belongs to a 'servant group', and has
a 'shepherd' and a 'caring brother or sister'.

The **Multiply Christian Network**, started in 1992, is a
partnership of about 25 independent churches and
groups, some in other countries.

Lutheran Church

Lutherans trace their history back to the beginnings of the Reformation, when Martin Luther was excommunicated by the Roman Catholic Church in 1521. Since then, it has spread to many parts of the world.

It is the state church in Germany (where it is called the Evangelical Church) and in the Scandinavian countries including Iceland. Being the state church means that often religious questions are settled in connection with the government. It is also very strong in the USA, where there are many Lutheran denominations, as there are in Europe. Organisation can vary considerably. Worldwide, they number over 80 million, with about three-quarters belonging to the Lutheran World Federation. Lutherans play a strong part in the ecumenical movement.

In Britain, the first church was formed in London in 1673. This was for the benefit of craftsmen who were brought in from Germany to help after the Great Fire of London in 1666. In the eighteenth century, the fact that King George I had been a German Lutheran encouraged many to come over with him. These included George F. Handel, the composer. In the 1930s when Hitler came to power, and particularly after World War II, Lutheran refugees flocked to Britain from Europe.

The Lutheran Council of Great Britain was formed in 1948. Their aim has been to have one Lutheran Church in place of the many different national groups which are now linked to the Council, e.g. German, Estonian, Latvian, Polish, Hungarian, Swedish, Finnish. The Evangelical Lutheran Church of England is independent from the Lutheran Council, and is affiliated to the Missouri Synod in the USA. Altogether, there are some 15,000 Lutherans in Britain.

Their teaching

Official teaching is found in the Book of Concord, which in effect sums up Martin Luther's teaching. The Bible is the supreme authority, to which creeds and statements of belief are all subordinated. Nevertheless, they make use of the historic creeds, the Augsburg Confession of 1530, and Luther's Small Catechism, which is used to instruct confirmation candidates.

'Justification by faith' is still central, that salvation can only be found by trusting Christ, and not through doing good works. This was the main plank of Luther's teaching and of the Reformation. Because of the Fall in the Garden of Eden, original righteousness was lost. Since then, all human beings have been in bondage to sin by nature. But, through Christ and his death on the cross to atone for sin, the sinner who trusts in Christ is now accounted righteous before God. It is all due to God's grace alone.

In their teaching about the return of Christ, they are usually Amillennial (p. 14), not believing in a literal thousand year reign of Christ on the earth.

A strong line is taken against Freemasonry.

In the eighteenth century, great inroads were made into the traditional Lutheran teaching by those who emphasised the importance of 'reason'. They downgraded the supernatural element in salvation. At the time, this was counteracted by the movement started by Count von Zinzendorf and the Moravian Brethren, known on the Continent as the Herrnhuters (see the Moravians (p. 94)). But then, in the nineteenth century, Lutheran scholars in Germany were prominent in the support of 'critical' teaching which said that much in the Bible could not be trusted. This has had a big influence not only in Lutheran circles, but also much further afield.

Their practice

Services are usually liturgical, with preaching playing a significant part. Infant baptism is normally the practice. Communion services are held with Luther's distinctive teaching of 'consubstantiation', i.e. that Christ's body and blood are there with the bread and wine, but do not replace them (as with Roman Catholic teaching on 'transubstantiation').

On the whole, churches are free to run their own affairs, electing their own pastors and other officers. Pastors may be men or women in the UK.

Messianic Jews

The Messianic Jews are those who have come to believe that Jesus is the Messiah, the anointed king foretold by the prophets, who honour him as Saviour and Lord, but feel called to worship in a particularly Jewish way. For both Jew and Gentile, salvation can only be through the atoning sacrifice of Jesus on the cross, and his resurrection is vital.

Although they acknowledge a spiritual oneness with Gentile Christians, they have a Jewish identity which they feel it would be wrong to lose. They are 'fulfilled Jews' rather than 'converted Christians'. In fact, some fight shy of calling themselves Christians at all, because of the misunderstanding this could cause in their families and in the Jewish community. As well as this, although wanting good relationships with Gentile Christians, they find that some can show a deep hostility. Anti-Semitism by certain 'Christians' is still a big issue.

It is important for them that God's covenant with the Jews, which started with Abraham, has not been revoked. This is why the Jews have survived as an identifiable people. Now the Messianic Jews see themselves as the 'remnant', because of whom 'Israel' will continue to survive. Because of this, they can also be a bridge between Jews and Christians.

The Messianic congregations

The movement began in Russia in the middle of the nineteenth century. In the USA, it blossomed in the 1960s when many Jews, who had been hippies, came to faith in Christ, and formed communities outside the mainline denominations. Now, many hundreds of these communities exist there, as well as over forty in Israel, with many in Eastern Europe and elsewhere.

In the British Isles, the Messianic congregations only started a few years ago. Over twenty have now been formed. Each one is autonomous and independent, and have different ideas, e.g. about how far to keep the food laws and Sabbath observances, whether to light candles in worship and wear the kippah (head covering). Some have a charismatic emphasis (p. 16). Most practise believers' baptism, saying that circumcision is a sign of their birth as Jews, baptism a sign of their new birth.

It is usual to keep the feasts of Passover, Pentecost and Tabernacles to celebrate their history; also the Feast of Purim, to remember how God intervened through Esther to save the Jews from being wiped out.

Jesus is commonly called Yeshua (Joshua) to emphasise his Jewishness, using the Hebrew form of the name, whereas 'Jesus' is Greek. 'Messiah' is also used instead of Christ, and 'Ruach ha-Kodesh' for the Holy Spirit.

The Bible is referred to in its three parts: the Torah (the Pentateuch), the HafTorah (the rest of the 'Old Testament') and the Brit hadashah (the 'New Testament').

They meet for worship on Saturday mornings, the Sabbath. Much of the worship is extempore, although they also use a prayer book. They sing the Shema from Deuteronomy 6, 'The Lord is one . . .' and end with a Communion service.

Methodism

It was on May 24th, 1738, that John Wesley (1703–91), a Church of England minister, 'felt his heart strangely warmed' at a meeting in a house off Aldersgate Street, London. 'I felt I did trust in Christ, in Christ alone for my salvation, and an assurance was given me that he had taken away my sins, even mine, and saved me from the law of sin and death.' This experience was so to revolutionize his life that he became one of the most effective preachers there has ever been. (Methodists still remember May 24th as 'Wesley Day'.)

For over fifty years, he travelled the country 'offering Christ', believing that people of all kinds could become Christians instantaneously through repentance and faith in Christ.

As well as a great preacher, he was also a great organizer. He started religious societies for the large numbers who became Christians through his own preaching and through other preachers whom he sent out, mostly laymen. The societies were meant only to supplement the regular services of the Church of England, not to compete with them. John Wesley stayed a member of the Church of England throughout his life, as did his brother Charles, whose hymns played a significant part in the growth of Methodism.

When the two brothers were students at Oxford, they belonged to a group known as the 'Holy Club'. The disciplined and systematic way of life of these students had earned them the name 'Methodists', and this name stuck to their later work.

The societies were organised in 'classes' of about twelve people, which met weekly. The leader of each class had to take pastoral responsibility for each member, making sure that they lived a 'holy' life, as well as collecting a penny from each one each week.

The first Methodist Conference was held in 1744. After this, the whole 'connexion' was arranged in a series of circuits, round which the travelling preachers used to go. Most of England was covered in ten years. Little headway was made in Scotland. In Wales, it was Calvinistic Methodism (p. 11) which prevailed (as distinct from Wesley's Arminianism). Methodism was introduced into Ireland in 1747. In America, it began about 1760, and spread rapidly, with Francis Asbury as the leading figure.

Developments and breakaways

The time came when Wesley felt it necessary to ordain some of his preachers. He believed he had the right to do so, because he was an 'elder', and in New Testament times bishops and elders were the same. He first ordained men in America, then in Scotland and England, particularly to enable them to take baptisms and Communion services. Church of England bishops decided not ordain them, mainly because these men were ready to preach anywhere, not just within parish boundaries. It was also because Wesley licensed buildings for preaching.

His action in ordaining these men was to lead, after his death, to a break with the Church of England. The

Methodist Church was founded. But then divisions arose amongst the Methodists themselves. New Churches were founded.

One was the Primitive Methodist Church. It came into being out of a remarkable open-air camp meeting on a hill called Mow Cop in Staffordshire in 1810. Great crowds gathered and were greatly affected through the preaching of Hugh Bourne, William Clowes and others. Other camp meetings were held, until the Methodist Conference forbade any more to take place. Bourne and Clowes were expelled with others, and formed the Primitive Methodists in 1811. This was largely made up of ordinary working people, and it attracted a great many more as the century progressed. Many of the first leaders of the Labour movement belonged to the 'Prims' (which is why many Trade Unions were organised as 'chapels', rather like the class meeting, even down to collecting a subscription each week).

Another new Church was formed in the West Country in 1815, the Bible Christians. William Bryan, their leader, was keen that much more freedom should be allowed. One of the most renowned of their number was Billy Bray, a Cornishman. Unconventional in all he did, he was an unusually effective evangelist.

The parent body was now known as the Wesleyan Methodists. They were more middle-class than the others. For most of the nineteenth century, Jabez Bunting was the dominant influence, a powerful speaker with great intellectual ability. He was too dictatorial for some, who left and started two other groups. Later, these joined together, forming the United Methodist Free Church.

Reunions came in the twentieth century, first of all in 1907. The Bible Christians and the United Methodist Free, with others, formed the United Methodist Church. Then in 1932, 'The Methodist Church of Great Britain' came into being as the Wesleyans, the Primitives and the United Methodists finally joined together.

Over the years, Methodism has spread to about 100 countries, and worldwide has about 26 million members, with some 375,000 in Great Britain and 18,000 in Ireland. Although Ireland has a separate Conference covering North and South (by far the majority of churches are in the North), they have very much the same organisation, rules, even the same variety of churches, as in Great Britain. In each country, churches are strongly involved with ecumenical discussion and activity.

Including Ireland, there are twenty other self-governing Conferences throughout the world, linked together in the World Methodist Council.

The Methodist Missionary Society works in many parts of the world, especially Africa, India, S.E. Asia and the West Indies.

Their church government

This is partly Presbyterian and partly Anglican. Local churches are grouped in 'circuits' of varying size. These are the most influential administrative units, rather like the Presbyteries in Scotland. Ministers are appointed to the circuit, not to an individual church, even though they are responsible for one or more churches in the circuit (usually more). One minister is the Superintendent. He presides over the Quarterly Meeting of the circuit. The aim is that the churches work together as a circuit. Ministers preach in all the churches, not just their own. In the first place, they are invited for five years, but this can be extended.

'Circuit Stewards' are lay people who work with the ministers for the well-being of the circuit. They are also involved in the choosing of new ministers.

The circuit has a list of 'local preachers', lay people who have been through a course of training and been approved. Many of them are preaching almost every Sunday. Ministers must qualify as local preachers before going to theological college. Lay evangelists are trained at Cliff College in Derbyshire.

Each church is run by a Church Council, partly elected and partly of those representing church organisations. Church Stewards help with the day-to-day leadership.

Church membership is for 'all those who confess Jesus Christ as Lord and Saviour, and accept the obligation to serve him in the life of the Church and the world'. Each member is put under the care of a class leader.

After the circuit, the next step up is the district, under the supervision of a full-time Chairman, rather like an Anglican bishop. The district synod meets twice a year, made up of ministers and lay people.

The final authority on all questions of faith and practice is the annual 'Conference', made up of an equal number of ministers and lay representatives. District Chairmen are appointed by the Conference, and ministers, who may be men or women, are ordained at that time. Technically, it is the Conference which appoints ministers to circuits. The President of the Conference is always a minister, and appointed for a year. The Vice-President is always a lay person.

Their worship

No set forms are laid down for the worship services. A Service Book contains orders of service, but these are only for guidance and do not have to be followed. The Communion service is where the Service Book is used more frequently. Communion takes place at least once a month.

A minister normally presides. But, in rare circumstances, a local preacher may be allowed to preside.

Infant baptism is practised. But if adult applicants for membership have not been baptised before, they must be baptised before being received into membership. However, those who have already been baptised as infants cannot be baptised as an adult.

The annual Covenant Service is held early in the New Year. It was instituted by John Wesley and is seen as an important time when vows are renewed, and a commitment given to live that year in a truly Christian way.

Ordinary worship services vary greatly from church to church. Many churches prefer the traditional format, with hymns (those by Charles Wesley coming frequently), prayers, Bible readings and sermon, all taken by the minister or local preacher. Some prefer a liturgical service, using a set form and responses. In recent years, many have adopted a more informal approach, singing new 'spiritual songs' as well as hymns, and allowing participation by the congregation, especially in prayer. Some churches have been affected by the charismatic renewal, and the gifts of the Spirit may be exercised.

The old class meeting does not really exist today. But a kind of continuation can be seen in the house fellowships, where the small group encourages deeper fellowship and Christian living is discussed.

A service for marriage after divorce may be allowed, but the minister must decide in each case, perhaps after consultation with other ministers.

Their teaching

Official teaching recognises the Bible as the 'supreme rule of faith and practice'. Ministers and lay preachers are committed to the doctrines contained in John Wesley's *Notes on the New Testament* and his *Standard Sermons*. This means that the beliefs are evangelical (p. 10) and Arminian (p. 12).

Wesley's theology was shaped by the fact that he was a practical theologian, and was passionately involved with mission and salvation. He preached the sovereignty of God, but not in such a way that human responsibility was left out. In a sense, each person had to co-operate with God. He agreed with the Calvinists that depravity was total, that sin had affected every area of personality and being. It was impossible to earn or achieve one's own salvation. But he also believed that God had given sufficient grace to every person so that each had the resources to repent and have faith in Christ. It was necessary for them to appropriate that grace. Christ's death on the cross had accomplished salvation for all, even if it was not accepted by all.

When faith was exercised, the Holy Spirit could give assurance of salvation immediately, as he himself had experienced, knowing that his sins had been forgiven. That was assurance for the present. But it was not assurance of ultimate salvation. It was possible to lose salvation if following Christ was not maintained.

That is why he stressed the ethics of grace, that a relationship with God must be seen in loving action towards others. Wesley believed that God raised up Methodism to spread 'scriptural holiness'. In his teaching about 'entire sanctification', he said that this could happen instantaneously when people were earnestly seeking it. It needed to be maintained by disciplined living. But all could be filled with the love of God. This would be seen in their love for the 'lost' in evangelism, and doing all they could for those in need.

Although this is still official Methodist teaching, it is not always held or taught in the churches. In fact, a wide variety of theology is found. Many would see themselves simply as Methodists, with a great love for the Church, without going into the theology too deeply. But as well as this, as in other denominations, three groupings can be seen:

(1) Those with a 'high' view of the Church, who stress the importance of the sacraments and of using a liturgy. 'The Methodist Sacramental Fellowship' seeks to encourage and give fellowship to them.

(2) Those with a 'liberal' theology (p. 9), who tend to play down biblical teaching, saying it is often in error and out of date. The reality of miracles and the supernatural are denied. They seek to get away from traditional doctrines and explore new ideas, with Jesus as a role model rather than a divine Saviour. They are in the forefront of Methodist social involvement, with a great concern for the poor and the disadvantaged. An organisation called 'Alliance of Radical Methodists' (ARM), although fairly small, aims to encourage the outlook of liberals through conferences and literature. They are 'opposed to fundamentalism', and say all people can be treated as children of God. They challenge traditional structures and believe interfaith dialogue is important. The Church should be concerned for all the oppressed and exploited.

(3) Those who have an 'evangelical' (p. 10) theology. Most of them would preach the same truths as Wesley did, even if in different terminology. They feel that Methodism generally has been concentrating too much on the social implications of the gospel, and missing out on the gospel itself.

Headway is a large pressure group which uses literature and conferences to encourage biblical thinking. Social and ethical issues are important, but not so important as the Wesleyan gospel of personal salvation through Christ. It is this, they say, which leads to revival on a personal level and in the Church. They continue to affirm 'The Four Alls of Methodism' — All people need to be saved. All people can be saved. All people can know themselves to be saved. All people can be saved to the uttermost.

Easter People is also an evangelical movement which attracts thousands to an annual holiday conference.

Their social and humanitarian work

This has been important in Methodism since the early days. John Wesley himself, apart from helping the poor and those in prison, was a strong supporter of the movement to ban the slave trade. William Booth, the founder of the Salvation Army, had been a Methodist minister. Many Methodists have gone into politics, both locally and nationally. They have played an important part in the Trade Union movement. The Church has tried to tackle the problems of the inner city. Amongst other social projects today, breaking down racial prejudice and caring for asylum seekers from abroad are high on their agenda. They are well known for speaking out about the dangers of gambling and alcohol.

'NCH Action for Children' and 'Methodist Homes for the Aged' have won high praise for their pioneer work.

A vigorous debate is taking place in the denomination about practising homosexuals. Conference has approved their 'participation and ministry in the Church'. However, many are opposed to their recognition, believing it to be against biblical teaching.

Moravian Church

This is one of the oldest of the Free Churches, withdrawing from the Roman Catholic Church in 1457, 60 years before Martin Luther and the Reformation. They had been inspired by the preaching of John Hus, martyred in 1415. Beginning in Bohemia (now part of the Czech Republic), it spread to Moravia and Poland. They gradually became known as Moravians, although their official name was Unitas Fratrum, 'The Unity (or Fellowship) of the Brethren'.

One of their greatest leaders was Count von Zinzendorf who encouraged them to carry out some remarkable missionary work. In 1732 their first missionaries went to the West Indies, 60 years before William Carey went to India. Missionaries who came to England soon afterwards had a profound influence on John and Charles Wesley, as well as on many others. Now there are Moravians in most parts of the world, with an 'evangelical (p. 10), educational and medical witness'.

'Settlements' were built in various places, a well-known one being at Pudsey, between Leeds and Bradford. From these bases, itinerant preachers rode on horseback all over the British Isles. They aimed not so much to found churches, but to preach the gospel, linking their converts to local churches. This is why there have never been many Moravian churches.

In the UK, membership is about 2500 in some 40 churches; worldwide, about 400,000, more than half being in North America.

Church practice

The Synod of each Province is the highest authority, made up of ministers and lay representatives. This elects a Provincial Elders' Conference (or Board) to oversee the affairs of the Province. No one person is given the title of head of the Church, because they believe that only Jesus Christ can ever be the Head. Bishops have a pastoral role, not an administrative authority, continuing the work they have been doing, but with extra responsibilities. Ministers may be men or women, officially called Presbyters or Deacons. Lay people play an important part.

At least one worship service each Sunday is liturgical, but in the liturgy there is opportunity for free prayer. Other services are more unstructured. Communion, usually monthly, is open to all Christians, and it often follows a simple meal, the 'Agape' or Lovefeast. During the final hymn, members shake hands with each other as a sign of their fellowship together.

Infant baptism is usual. 'We declare that our children share with us the benefits of our Lord's redeeming work, and we claim them for the following of Christ as members of His Body, the Church.' Adult baptism is only for those not baptised in infancy. At confirmation, a personal confession is given of faith in Christ as Lord and Saviour. This leads to membership of the Church.

The Bible is the supreme authority for belief and conduct, the Apostles' and Nicene Creeds having a lesser place. One of their great emphases is on fellowship. 'Without fellowship there can be no Christianity.' They address each other as 'sisters' and 'brothers', members of a family.

The other great emphasis is on practical living. They declare themselves more concerned for 'conduct than creed'. They prefer to stress what Christians have in common, rather than what divides them. Nevertheless everything centres in Christ, 'who was crucified for our sin, and for our justification raised up from the dead. Whatsoever is contrary to this doctrine is contrary to our salvation.'

They believe that commitment to Christ is a commitment to serve sacrificially. That was the motive of their pioneer missionaries. Every Christian should be a servant, ready to go anywhere and do anything for God and their fellowmen.

They are fully committed to the Ecumenical Movement (p. 15), wanting to witness to 'the unity of all Christians and all the Churches in the fellowship of Christ'.

New Apostolic Church

Edward Irving (1792–1834) was a Presbyterian minister, and in the 1820s was the most eloquent and popular preacher in London. He came to believe that the Second Coming of Christ was very near, and in preparation for that, God was reviving the supernatural gifts of the Spirit and the offices of apostles and prophets. The first Apostle was appointed in 1832. After Irving's death in 1834, inspired by his teaching, the Catholic Apostolic Church was formed. In all, twelve apostles were appointed. Each one was assigned one or more countries, and went there as a missionary.

As time went by, they were influenced by certain Roman Catholic doctrines and practices. The name was changed to the New Apostolic Church. In the UK, it has about 2000 members in some 40 churches. Worldwide, it is active in 170 countries, with about 40,000 congregations and 6 million members. The headquarters is in Zurich, Switzerland.

Their teaching

They believe that it was only in 1832 that God sent apostles for the first time since the days of the New Testament. Until then, the Christian 'Church' had been a widow, with no children of God, because it is only through true Apostles that anybody can become a child of God. Jesus, as the Son of God, took the sins of mankind on himself, making possible a perfect reconciliation between man and God. Now, the offer of forgiveness for sin is made through the apostles. Those who receive this offer are being prepared for the imminent return of Christ, referred to as 'the First Resurrection'. They are his Bride, if they remain faithful.

After Christ's return, a thousand years of blessing on earth will take place (the Millennium), when the gospel will be offered to all. Then Satan will finally be defeated, judgment will be given, and those 'whose names are written in the Lamb's Book of Life by the Lord's Apostles' will share in the new heaven and the new earth.

Their organisation

The world leader is the Chief Apostle. Under him are district apostles, assisted by apostles, bishops and district leaders. The College of Apostles has the final authority for belief and practice, and they meet at intervals during the year. The UK branch is part of the Apostle District of Canada, and their apostle is in New York. Congregations are run by rectors, along with priests, deacons and subdeacons. All ministers are laymen and nearly all serve in an honorary capacity, being unpaid.

The sacraments

The three sacraments are vital:

(1) Holy baptism, which is in the name of the Trinity. It washes away inherited sin, and is seen as the first step

towards rebirth and fellowship with God. It is given to people of all ages, from children to adults. The water has to be consecrated first, and those baptised consecrate themselves to live as friends of God.

(2) Holy sealing. Those on whose heads the apostle's hands are laid receive the Holy Spirit through prayer, are born again and become members of the Church.

(3) Holy Communion. This is celebrated every Sunday by a priestly officeholder. The wafer of unleavened bread containing three drops of wine, after being blessed, becomes the body and blood of Jesus.

Their worship services have a simple liturgy. Preaching is always without notes, relying on the Holy Spirit. Choirs play an important part.

New Churches or House Church Movement

This title embraces a wide variety of churches, most of which belong to one of many different networks. These networks are independent, but their beliefs and practice are very similar to each other. At one time, they were quite tight-knit, working together. Now, having grown larger, they operate more independently, although the leaders have discussions together from time to time.

'Restoration Churches' is the name by which they have often been known. But 'New Churches' is now the way they prefer to be called. In fact, many of them are long established, and many have their own buildings. Others meet in community centres or school premises. Among them today are New Frontiers International, Ichthus, Pioneer People, Cornerstone Ministries, Covenant Ministries, Salt and Light, Plumbline, Outpouring Ministries, Community Resources.

The movement emerged in the early 1970s. Significant leaders have been Gerald Coates, Barney Coombes, Peter Fenwick, Roger Forster, Bryn Jones, Tony Morton, John Noble, David Tomlinson, Terry Virgo and, very much the inspiration in the early days, Arthur Wallis. Their growth has been quite spectacular. Membership in the UK is well over 100,000 with a number of individual churches having congregations of over 1000.

Restoration

As a development of the charismatic movement (p. 16), with its emphasis on personal renewal by the Holy Spirit, they believed there was a need also to restore the pattern of church life as far as possible to that of the New Testament church, with particular emphasis on a new freedom in worship, strong relationships between members, leaders in covenant relationship with each other, the practice of all spiritual gifts and of all the ministries of Ephesians 4:11, including apostles and prophets. Because of their lack of 'tradition', they see themselves as having liberty to move and change as they feel led. Thus the situation is continually changing. New initiatives are always being explored.

At one time, they looked down on denominations, and felt they alone were in the will of God. Gradually that viewpoint has mellowed, and now most leaders have good relationships with those in the mainline denominations, especially with those who are evangelical, sometimes working with them.

The main leaders are in a sense all laymen, although they work full-time and are paid. Ordination does not take place. They try to have as little central administration as possible, leaving authority to make decisions in the hands of local pastors and elders.

As with many other evangelical churches (p. 10), they believe that membership of the local church is only for those who have experienced the new birth, and who are baptised in water as believers. They emphasise the need to be baptised in the Holy Spirit, who equips each member with spiritual gifts to be used for the common good.

Their worship

Worship services, often lasting two or three hours, are lively, with much singing, especially of modern 'spiritual songs'. No liturgy is used. The leading is very informal. Members of the congregation may be called upon at any time to contribute, and testimonies may be given of healing, etc. Time may be allowed for the gifts of the Spirit to be exercised, particularly in smaller meetings. In larger meetings, the worship is more structured. The preaching may last an hour.

The pattern of meetings generally has followed that of cell, congregation and celebration (as other churches do, mainly charismatic). The cell is a meeting in the home, usually during the week, perhaps a dozen people, with opportunity for fellowship and pastoral care. Congregations are larger, serving an area, holding Sunday worship, and serving as a base for evangelism and social action. The celebration is when, from time to time, a number of congregations come together, giving the sense of a big occasion.

Church life

Their teaching about the kingdom of God, that lives must be submitted to Christ in every way, means that church fellowship is seen as a total way of life. Each member is expected to contribute spiritually and practically. Home groups provide the main opportunity for this. All material possessions are expected to be available as needed, and giving is generous, a high proportion going to overseas missions and humanitarian work.

Firm control is exercised by leaders. Apostles have responsibilities for a number of churches, giving vision and guidance. This may include appointing elders. They do not claim to be on a par with the original Twelve Apostles, but are men whom local church leaders recognise, and to whom they voluntarily relate and defer. Apostles usually work with teams of men responsible to them, who help in the oversight of churches.

Apostles also take the lead in church planting, e.g. New Frontiers International, based in Brighton, has oversight of about 140 churches, about half of them planted by themselves; Ichthus, based in South London, has about 150 churches linked to them, many of which they have planted; Pioneer, based in Cobham, Surrey, have about 100; Covenant Ministries, based in Coventry, have over 60; Cornerstone Ministries, based in Southampton, have helped to establish over 30 churches.

They also believe that the office of prophet is being restored today, men or women who bring God's clear word of direction for the church and for individuals. They cannot add to Scripture or cut across the clear teaching of Scripture.

To encourage unity and maturity at the local level, there is a voluntary submission by members to leaders, especially to elders. In some fellowships, there is also a carefully worked-out arrangement where each member is spiritually responsible to and for someone else, a kind of pyramid structure often known as 'shepherding'. Differences of opinion exist as to how strongly this authority should be exercised. Some apostolic teams encourage obedience to those over them much more than others. Criticism has sometimes been levelled because leaders have been over-zealous in this way, have been too autocratic and intolerant of disagreement. They admit that 'discipling' can go wrong, but say that when exercised in love and sensitivity, it can give strength and security, leading to changed lives.

Deacons are agents of the eldership, with some specific area of responsibility. Most groups prefer male leadership, but some, such as Ichthus, have women leaders as well.

As well as engaging in vigorous evangelism and in missionary work abroad, the churches are also involved with humanitarian and social work here and in poor countries, for example running a hospice for AIDS sufferers in Romania and a maternity hospital in Zambia. In the UK they run homes for single mothers, pregnancy counselling services, projects for the unemployed and for housing, helping AIDS sufferers, a credit bank, etc.

The bride

There has been teaching that before Christ returns, there will be a worldwide revival, with a great coming together of all churches, restored in the same way as their own have been. The Church would then be a spotless bride fit to welcome the King. This teaching has been toned down to some extent, as it has been realised that God can work in other church structures. But some leaders still feel that unity must come in some way, and that an outpouring of God's Spirit throughout the world will take place before the return of Christ. This will mean a time of peace, when spiritual and earthly authorities will be subdued. Other leaders are unsure about this teaching, such as Roger Forster of Ichthus, who is a premillennialist (p. 14), and believes that Christ could return at any time.

Orthodox Churches

In AD 330, the Roman Emperor Constantine made Byzantium his new capital. He called it Constantinople (now Istanbul in Turkey). A Christian community was already there, and now Constantinople became the great centre of Christian influence in the East, as Rome was in the West. Over the centuries, the split widened between the Catholic West and the Orthodox East. ('Orthodox' here means much more 'correct worship' rather than 'correct belief'.)

The split finally took definite form in 1054, when the Church of Rome excommunicated the Eastern Church. The main reason was their refusal to accept the Pope's authority over the whole Church. Amongst other disagreements, the East did not accept the Catholic teaching about purgatory, nor that the Holy Spirit 'proceeded' from the Son of God as well as the Father. (This is often known as the Filioque Clause. *Filioque* is the Latin word for 'and from the Son', which the Catholic Church added to the Creed without consulting the Eastern churches.)

The Orthodox churches view the Pope as only the head of one particular Church, like their own patriarchs and archbishops. Over the years, the two Churches have tried to ignore each other, or have tried to force the other into submission.

The two families

Today, Orthodoxy is made up of many self-governing Churches, but each of them belongs to one of two families, the Eastern and the Oriental Orthodox. The Eastern is much larger, with twenty national churches in communion with the Ecumenical Patriarch of Constantinople, who is seen as the first among equals. The Oriental only have five churches, but they are older. They are in Egypt (Coptic, 8 million adherents, Syria, Armenia, India and Ethiopia, which has 15 million).

By far the biggest of the Eastern churches is the Russian, with about 70 million. But other large ones are the Romanian (17 million), Bulgarian and Greek (both 8 million). There are close ties between them all.

Worldwide, the Orthodox Community numbers about 140 million. The UK estimate is nearly 290,000, with about 270,000 of these being Greek Orthodox. But the parishes, mostly in England, come under the jurisdiction of a number of both Eastern and Oriental churches.

The two families do not now have much disagreement, but are not officially 'in communion'. One difference is that the Oriental Churches believe Christ had only one nature (known as Monophysitism) whereas the Eastern Churches, along with mainstream Christianity, believe that he had both a divine and a human nature. Otherwise both families have more or less the same beliefs and the same kind of worship.

The head of each Church is one of their bishops. He may be given the title of Patriarch or Metropolitan or Archbishop or Exarch, etc. The title shows his seniority, but all bishops are counted as equal to one another, and they believe they can 'trace their descent by uninterrupted succession from the Apostles'. Each bishop has a diocese. A priest, or more than one, runs the parishes. A priest can be married, but cannot be a woman. Laymen play an active role in the parishes.

Their teaching

The Church derives its teaching from both 'Holy Scripture and Sacred Tradition', which they see as of equal value. They complete each other. The 'Sacred Tradition' includes the decisions of the seven Ecumenical Councils. The Nicene Creed is central to their faith.

However, dogmatic theology is not a priority. They fight shy of definition as much as possible, not wanting to be too rational. They have a more mystical approach, emphasising the mystery of God. Although God has revealed himself, yet it is never possible to have a complete knowledge of him. For them, worship is adoring the mystery, not trying to understand too much.

They have two major beliefs:

(1) The Trinity, with three Persons in one Godhead.
(2) The Incarnation of the Second Person of the Trinity.

The Church is there 'for the salvation of man, bearing His holy sanction and authority'. They believe the Holy Spirit speaks to each member, and every Christian has to hear for himself. So, for instance, no law is laid down about contraception, although they teach the moral consequences of using artificial means.

Salvation is seen, not so much as a release from sin and its consequences, but as freedom from death. Immortality and holiness are given as a result of Christ's victory over the powers of evil through his resurrection. Because of their strong emphasis on the resurrection, they prefer the empty cross as the symbol of faith, rather than the crucifix.

It is very important to them that the Church is seen as including Christians who have died, that they are still in fellowship with those who are living. And they themselves have a strong sense of belonging to one another in the body of Christ.

Their worship

Worship is their great priority. They have an 'eternal liturgy' — it has not changed for over a thousand years. Preaching and reading from the Bible must lead primarily to worship. The purpose of mission is to bring all people to worship the Trinity. When individual Christians worship, they become fully the Church.

The church buildings are different from those in the West. They are roughly square inside, so that the people will feel involved as they stand together for what may be a long service. Over them is a dome, which is crowned with golden eight-pointed crosses, a symbol of Christ's victory over death. Outside, the building may be unadorned, quite plain. But inside, it is beautifully decorated. This symbolises going from the world to heaven through the worship.

A solid screen, the Iconastasis, separates the nave (where the people stand) from the east end of the building. The area behind this screen is called the altar, and it is there that the Communion table, the 'holy table', 'the throne', stands. The clergy spend most of the service behind the screen, which represents the division between heaven and earth, brought about because people have turned away from God.

On the screen are icons, pictures painted on wood, mostly of saints who have died and are now in heaven. The icons are there to be a stimulus and an encouragement to worship and to holy living.

In the middle of the screen is a large pair of doors, the Holy or Royal Doors, which open and shut at different stages of the service, when the priest or deacon appears. (A deacon is the first stage in becoming a priest.)

Worship, for the Orthodox, is not just for the mind and heart, but for the body as well. Through worship, bodies and souls are brought into sacramental union with the risen Christ. To help in this way:

- the sign of the cross is often made, and they bow before Christ;
- the Book of the Gospels is carried round the building;
- some may fall on their knees, symbolising repentance;
- a lot of movement, even dancing, may take place;
- candles are lit, to represent Christ as the light of the world;
- incense is used, symbolising prayer;
- icons and frescoes on the screen and walls may represent Jesus, Mary, the saints, scenes from the Bible, showing what Christ can do in people's lives.

Worship can be rich and colourful. It may be long and solemn, or it can be full of joy, especially at Easter. The priest mostly faces the same way as the congregation, praying with them. The deacon moves between the altar and the people, leading prayers and singing, helping the priest. The choir sings.

At times, hymns and prayers are in honour of Mary. She is above the saints, because she is the Mother of God, the Mother of the Incarnate Word, the Most Holy.

The services

Although many different services are held, the most important one is on Sunday mornings, 'The Divine Liturgy' or

Eucharist, the Communion service. Vespers is celebrated on Saturday evenings, as part of the preparation.

In the first part, they worship together, hear the Scriptures being read and receive instruction. In the second part, they recite the Nicene Creed and have prayers of thanksgiving. Then the priest comes through the doors to the people with the bread and wine, which have been given by the people themselves. Leavened bread is used, and red wine with hot water added. The priest takes them round the church and back to the table, where he offers them up to God. Then he takes them to the altar steps where the people receive them.

During the service, Christ's life is remembered from his coming down from heaven through to his ascension. But it is not merely a memorial. It is Christ, the High Priest, present with his people and offering to the Father his once-for-all sacrifice of his own body and blood on their behalf. So the people participate in his one eternal sacrifice, and become worthy to stand before God.

The sacraments ('The Holy Mysteries')

Although there are many sacraments, these are the most important:

(1) *Baptism.* It is usually infants who are baptised. The priest completely immerses the infants three times in the water, baptising them in the name of the Father, the Son and the Holy Spirit. A fresh white garment is put on them, and each is given a baptismal name of one of the saints. Through baptism, they are given spiritual life and enter into the church community.

(2) *Chrismation (or Confirmation).* This follows immediately after baptism. Various parts of the head and

body are anointed with special oil (chrism). In this way, the gift of the Holy Spirit is received, and other sacraments can be taken. Now there is also the right later on to teach and take responsibility in the Church.

(3) *Communion*. After baptism and chrismation, infants are able to receive Communion at the Eucharist, the Divine Liturgy, when it is believed, the bread and wine become the body and blood of Christ.

(4) *Confession*. The priest represents the whole Church, as he and the penitent stand facing a table with the Book of the Gospels and a cross. The priest is not a judge, only a witness, and afterwards pronounces forgiveness, leading to reconciliation to God and the Church.

(5) *Holy Unction (Anointing of the Sick)*. This may be for psychological as well as for physical ailments. The priest and members of the church gather round, and together pray for healing. The priest then anoints with oil.

(6) *Marriage*. This is called 'The Crowning', because at the wedding, the couple are first of all crowned, after which the crowns are held above their heads for the rest of the service. No promises are made, but they express their consent to marry each other. Rings are exchanged, and a cup of wine shared. The Church does not really approve of divorce or remarriage. But a bishop may allow divorce in certain circumstances. Remarriage can then take place in the church.

(7) *Ordination*. The local congregation starts the process. After the candidate has been trained, the bishop ordains him during the Divine Liturgy by laying hands on his head. He now becomes a deacon, later becoming a priest, when he is ordained again.

Festivals

Many festivals take place during the year. Those which celebrate the baptism of Christ and his transfiguration are especially popular. But it is Easter that is the 'feast of feasts', the crown of the year. The congregation process round the church until they come to the main door, which is closed, a symbol of the sealed tomb. The priest shouts 'Christ is risen', the door is opened, and inside a blaze of light greets them from every lamp and candle, symbolising the opening of the tomb. The priest goes round shouting, 'Christ is risen', and the people take up the cry, 'He is risen indeed'. There is much rejoicing.

Special services can be held in church or home, e.g. because of a new job, or going on a journey, or for blessings received. Houses, gardens, crops, animals can be blessed by the Church.

The home

Many homes have family prayers at the 'icon corner', where icons of Christ and Mary are central. Round them are icons of saints. The Gospels are read and explained. Prayers are read from the prayer book. Hymns are sung.

The monasteries

Monks and nuns choose a life of celibacy, poverty and obedience. Different countries specialise in different types of work. But prayer is the main work. Retreats are often held in the monasteries. The centre of the whole monastic system is Mount Athos in Greece. On this peninsula, there are twenty self-governing monasteries.

Pentecostalism

During the last 50 years, the Pentecostals have been growing faster throughout the world than any other church or
denomination. In 1960, for instance, they numbered 12
million; in 1995, 106 million. In 1960, 1% of the Christian
community; now 7%, and expecting to advance on that.

Literally hundreds of different groups are called Pentecostal, probably over a thousand. This name is used because it is believed they are in line with the events on the
day of Pentecost, as recorded in Acts 2. As with 'charismatic' (p. 16) teaching in other churches, they say there is
an experience known as 'the baptism in the Holy Spirit'
which comes to Christian believers. It gives new spiritual
power both for service in the Church and for witness to
the world. This experience leads to the 'gifts of the Spirit'
being exercised in the Church. These gifts include speaking with other tongues, prophecy and healing, which God
gives for building up the Church.

'Pentecostal' movements have arisen before in church
history, such as the Montanists in the second century and
the Irvingites in the nineteenth century. But modern Pentecostalism began in Los Angeles in 1906. A negro
preacher, W.J. Seymour, hired an old Methodist chapel,
and through his preaching about the baptism of the Spirit,
'the fire came down'. For three years, prayer meetings took

place with speaking and singing in tongues, and prophecy. The movement spread. People from round the world came to see what was happening, and returned home, having received an experience and a message.

In Britain, it is usually said that Pentecostalism started in Sunderland in 1907. It is true that many individuals had had an experience of the Spirit in the Welsh Revival of 1904/5, and gifts of the Spirit were exercised then. Some who later became powerful leaders of the Pentecostal movement were deeply affected at that time, including the Jeffreys brothers and Donald Gee. But it was at All Saints Church in Sunderland that the movement burst into life.

T.B. Barratt had had an experience in Los Angeles, and was invited to Sunderland by the All Saints' Vicar, Alexander Boddy, who himself had worked with Evan Roberts, the most influential figure of the Welsh Revival. So much happened in Sunderland that Alexander Boddy became central in the spread of Pentecostal teaching in Britain, and his parish a mecca for the great numbers who came seeking the Pentecostal experience. It was there that Smith Wigglesworth, a Bradford plumber, had an experience which turned him into a Pentecostal ambassador all round the world, preaching to vast crowds.

For some years, Pentecostals stayed in their own churches and denominations. In 1909 the Pentecostal Missionary Union was founded, and gave some sort of cohesion to the movement. Two of its leaders were Alexander Boddy and Cecil Polhill, an Etonian squire who had been a missionary in Tibet, going out with the 'Cambridge Seven'.

Gradually the mainstream evangelical churches in Britain turned against the Pentecostals. This was partly because some extremists gave the movement a bad name. But it was also because Pentecostals tended to condemn the churches in strong language, saying they had betrayed

Christ and seeming to suggest that nothing had happened in church history between the Acts of the Apostles and Azusa Street.

Thus it was inevitable that Pentecostal churches were formed, but they were on the fringe of the evangelical world until recent years, when they have moved more into the mainstream. The three main groups (apart from the black-led Pentecostal churches) are: the Apostolic Church, which arose out of the Welsh Revival as separate churches merged together; Elim, which in a sense started in 1915, although the name came later; and the Assemblies of God which started in 1924, when the Pentecostal Missionary Union came to an end.

The black-led Pentecostal churches began to appear in the 1950s, to a large extent because of immigration. See 'Afro-Caribbean and Black-led Churches' (page 19).

Their church life

Worship is of a lively and enthusiastic nature, with rousing singing. People who are used to traditional services may find them too emotional. The Communion service is usually held every Sunday, and the congregation participate, with the gifts of the Spirit often being exercised. It may be that everyone will speak in tongues together and pray at the same time.

When people are ill, prayer is made for their healing, with hands being laid upon them. It is believed that healing is important to show God's power today. Many Pentecostals would say that 'healing is in the atonement', that just as Christ died for the sins of all, so his healing is for all, and can be claimed. Not everybody would agree with this, although the idea that illness is 'the work of Satan' is a common belief. Deliverance from demons may also take place. Services feature testimonies of healing and conversion.

Preaching is biblically based, and can be forceful and emotional. The sermons may well bring out the Pentecostal emphasis on the **Foursquare Gospel**, i.e. that Christ is the Saviour, Baptiser in the Holy Spirit, Healer and Coming King. A regular theme too is that the Second Coming of Christ is imminent, based on their Premillennial (p. 14) understanding that Christ will reign on the earth for a thousand years.

In the past, Pentecostal preachers have been criticised for being too superficial, exhorting, emphasising the experience side of the Christian life with not enough teaching on doctrine. This is now changing. Pastors are given a full theological training, and biblical teaching has a much higher profile. Nevertheless, they are very much against critical scholarship and liberal theology (p. 9), believing strongly that the Bible is the inspired Word of God.

The need to live a holy life by biblical standards is always being stressed. The disciplined life is often spelt out, for example, keeping away from tobacco, alcohol, drugs and secular dancing. Members are expected to observe Sunday as the Sabbath day, and to give a tithe, a tenth, of their income.

Most Pentecostals in this country see sanctification (p. 12), the growth in holiness, as a continuous work in the believer, the baptism in the Spirit giving added impetus. Some support a kind of 'holiness teaching' which speaks of sanctification as a third experience. Baptism is by immersion, and limited to those who profess faith in Christ. A service of dedication is held for babies. Immediately after people have been baptised as believers, it is usual to lay hands on them, that they may receive the baptism of the Holy Spirit.

The local church membership is only open to those who are 'born of the Holy Spirit' and have faith in Christ. All members should be concerned about evangelism, and many people are attracted by the warmth of fellowship in the churches.

The teaching about salvation is Arminian (p. 12), that God has given to all the grace they need to repent and have faith in Christ. But salvation can be lost. In recent years, interest has grown in Reformed (p. 11) theology, although this is not widely held.

Women can be pastors in Elim and the Assemblies of God, but in practice there are only a few. Women cannot be pastors in the Apostolic Church.

Lay elders have had an increasingly important role alongside the pastor in spiritual leadership.

Much social and humanitarian work takes place, especially in the inner city. Pentecostal churches have been known for reaching out to those unreached by other churches.

National and international conventions are held frequently. In the UK, 'The Pentecostal Churches of the British Isles' links the denominations loosely. Particularly close ties exist between AOG and Elim. None of them is involved with the ecumenical movement.

The Apostolic Church

This church grew out of the 1904 Welsh Revival, and its headquarters is still at Penygroes in South Wales. As a result of the Revival, certain churches were exercising the gifts of the Spirit, and some believed that God was also restoring the roles of apostles and prophets. These churches gradually merged. The first leader of the combined fellowship was Daniel Powell Williams, ordained an Apostle in 1913, and becoming first President of the Apostolic Church Council. He remained so until his death in 1947.

In their understanding, there are two kinds of ministers. The ascension ministers are the five referred to in Ephesians 4:11 — apostles, prophets, evangelists, pastors and teachers. These are not limited to ministry in the local church. A pastor, for example, will often cover more than one church. However, the local ministers are elders, deacons and deaconesses, who work only in one church.

The apostles are the highest authority in the Church. They hold their office for life, and all are equal. Their responsibilities include clarifying doctrinal matters and having the sole power to call, ordain and place the ministers. Apostles minister at National, Regional, Area and District level.

The General Council takes major decisions for the Church. The Council comprises all apostles and representatives of other ascension ministries. They may be helped by prophetic utterances, but these are not looked on as infallible.

At the local level, the church is governed by pastors and elders, known as the Presbytery. Members must be baptised believers, and at least 14 years old. They cannot belong to a secret society such as the Freemasons. In the services, all are encouraged to participate in prayer and praise, exercising spiritual gifts.

Divorce can only be on the ground of sexual immorality. Adultery and homosexual practice are condemned.

Their statement of faith is called 'The Tenets of the Church'. Basically evangelical (p. 10), they speak, for example of 'The utter depravity of human nature, the necessity of repentance and regeneration, and the eternal doom of the finally impenitent'.

They also speak of 'The Baptism of the Holy Spirit for believers, with signs following', and 'The Nine Gifts of the

Holy Ghost for the edification, exhortation and comfort of the Church, which is the Body of Christ'. One Tenet speaks of Christ's 'Second Coming and Millennial Reign on earth'. Also, 'the possibility of falling from grace'.

The Church has expanded to every continent through the Apostolic Missionary movement. In each of 40 countries, the Church operates on an independent basis, being linked together through the Apostolic Fellowship. Worldwide, membership is about 4.5 million, with some 5000 in the UK.

Elim Foursquare Gospel Alliance

The name comes from the Foursquare Gospel — Christ as saviour, baptiser in the Holy Spirit, healer and coming King.

Two brothers were amongst the most remarkable leaders of early Pentecostalism — George and Stephen Jeffreys. Their father was a miner in Maesteg, South Wales. While still in their twenties, they were preaching to thousands. In 1915, George founded the Elim Evangelistic Band to help with the huge evangelistic missions in Wales, Ireland and England. In 1926, he formed the Elim Foursquare Gospel Alliance with the hope that it would become an umbrella organisation for all Pentecostals. In fact, those who joined were only those who had been with him before.

In the 1930s, tension arose between George and the other leaders. He felt the movement was being too centralised and organised, and his authority was curtailed. In 1939 he left to form the Bible Pattern Church Fellowship.

Elim have a centralised form of government on presbyterian (p. 7) lines. The Annual Conference is the final authority for faith and practice, and it consists of an equal number of ministerial and lay representatives. The country is divided into seven Regions, each with a Superintendent, with a General Superintendent over all. The Regions are divided into Presbyteries. Local churches have pastors (male or female), elders and deacons, who form the Church Session and have the oversight of the church.

The 'Fundamental Truths' include: 'We believe . . . that the believer is promised an enduement of power as the gift of Christ through the baptism of the Holy Spirit with signs following'. As distinct from the Assemblies of God, they do not believe that speaking in tongues is the only 'initial evidence' of being baptised in the Holy Spirit.

They have a firm belief that the ministries of apostles, prophets, evangelists, pastors and teachers are for today; and also that 'the gospel embraces the needs of the whole man and that the Church is therefore commissioned to preach the gospel to the world and to fulfil a ministry of healing and deliverance to the spiritual and physical needs of mankind'.

Membership is nearly 70,000 in the UK.

Assemblies of God

It was said previously that in the early years, most Pentecostals continued to belong to their own churches, although linked to some extent through the Pentecostal Missionary Union. Then, finding they were not accepted, they began to form their own churches. In 1924, the Assemblies of God was founded to bring them together, as well as taking over from the PMU. The churches had started independently, and did not want to lose their independence. About 70 assemblies joined.

Evangelistic and healing campaigns continued to attract great crowds with men like Stephen Jeffreys and

Smith Wigglesworth. In Britain, the AOG remained comparatively small compared with Scandinavia, Italy and France. It may be because many of the best people became missionaries abroad. And often, the early pastors were only part-time, with little training.

Donald Gee (1891–1966) did more than anyone to raise the standards of preaching and church life generally. He was known as a Bible teacher in many parts of the world, and wrote extensively. In 1948, he became Chairman of AOG, as well as being in charge of their Bible School. He and David du Plessis did much to encourage good relationships with other Churches.

Pastors are now well trained, both men and women. In the local church, they are helped by elders and deacons.

The UK is organised into twelve regions, each with a superintendent. A general superintendent oversees the whole work. The Annual General Conference is the final authority. Conferences and seminars are held to give teaching and encourage fellowship. Church Planting Teams are sent out. Homes for the elderly and a Child Care Association are among the social action projects. Missionaries work in Europe, Africa and the Far East. Membership numbers 60,000 in the UK.

The 'Statement of Fundamental Truths' includes: 'We believe in the baptism in the Holy Spirit, the initial evidence of which is the speaking with other tongues as the Spirit gives utterance.' 'We believe that deliverance from sickness by Divine Healing is provided for in the Atonement.'

Life and Light

In Europe and America, a remarkable Pentecostal movement has recently been taking place among gypsies. As a result of this, gypsy churches have been formed, in Britain through the mission called Life and Light, now affiliated to the Assemblies of God. The latest figure quoted was 25 churches, but now there may be many more. It is said that many thousands of gypsies have become Christians, and pastors are being trained to look after them. Evangelism is the great priority, with teams of workers going to places where gypsies gather.

Meetings in the churches are exuberant, characterised by enthusiastic singing and informality. Testimonies are given of what God has been doing. Preaching is down-to-earth. One important outcome of the movement is that the old suspicions between different groups of gypsies are being removed.

Oneness Pentecostals

Some Pentecostal groups do not believe in the traditional teaching about the Trinity. They are known as 'Oneness Pentecostals' or 'Jesus Only' or 'Jesus-Name Pentecostals'. Ideally, they should be called Unitarian Pentecostals. In the UK, there are some 19 groups, many among the black-led churches. Ministers are often part-time.

Their teaching is that God is one Person who shows himself as Father in creation, the Son in redemption and the Holy Spirit in emanation. The Father of the Old Testament and the Holy Spirit are no more than alternative forms in which the Christ who appeared in Jesus is manifested. Water baptism is only valid if carried out in the name of Jesus alone.

The largest of these groups in Britain is the United Pentecostal Church with about 3000 members. Their Annual Conference of ministers alone is the final authority for belief and practice. Churches have pastors and deacons. The churches are linked by districts, which have superintendents and presbyters. A General Superintendent and a General Board supervises the Church nationally. Believers are baptised by full immersion 'In the name of Jesus Christ for the remission of sins'.

Presbyterianism

It was John Calvin in Geneva who laid the foundations of Presbyterianism in the sixteenth century. He established its organisation and its theology. The movement quickly spread, first of all in every direction across Europe. Then, over the succeeding centuries, it became the most widespread of all Protestant movements, taking root in at least 100 countries, and now having some 48 million members. Where the churches are called 'Reformed', e.g. the Dutch Reformed Church, it means they have originated on the continent of Europe. Where they are known as 'Presbyterian', e.g. the Presbyterian Church, USA, it shows they have originated in the English-speaking world.

Although there is a multiplicity of Presbyterian denominations, with each of them being self-governing, most of them are linked to the 'World Alliance of Reformed Churches', which meets every four years for discussion. From here, advice is given to the churches, but it has no actual authority. Presbyterians have always been in the forefront of the ecumenical movement (p. 15), although some denominations are opposed to it.

Presbyterianism is particularly strong in the USA, Canada, Australia, New Zealand and South Africa, as well as Scotland, Northern Ireland and Wales. In England, it has never been strong since the mid-1600s, and in

1972 the English Presbyterian Church joined with the Congregationalists to form the United Reformed Church.

The movement came to the UK first of all through John Knox (1514–72). Although a Scotsman, he had been a minister in England, but had fled to Geneva when Mary became Queen in 1553. There he had met John Calvin and had embraced his teaching. Returning to Scotland in 1555, his preaching and writing made a powerful impression. By 1560, the Reformation was officially accepted in Scotland.

In the mid-1600s, it seemed that England would become Presbyterian as well as Scotland. The Westminster Confession of Faith, very much a Presbyterian document, was completed in 1646, and approved by Parliament. But when the Restoration came with Charles II, the Act of Uniformity of 1662 meant the return to dominance of the Church of England. Many hundreds of Presbyterian (and other) ministers were ejected from their parishes in both England and Scotland. Presbyterianism was only restored to Scotland in 1690, after much persecution.

In Northern Ireland, the movement was strengthened in the early 1600s, as the government planted many settlers from Scotland.

The Evangelical Revival of the eighteenth century had a greater impact in Wales than in England. It was during this time that the Presbyterian Church in Wales was founded, often known as the Calvinistic Methodists.

In Scotland, splinter groups kept breaking away and forming new denominations (although many have been reunited since). But the most far-reaching was in 1843, when about a third of the ministers, nearly 500, left the Church of Scotland and formed the Free Church of Scotland. It became known as 'the Great Disruption'. A number of factors were involved, the main one being that the civil courts insisted ministers should be appointed to parishes, even if the parishioners did not want them.

Those who left felt this was an intolerable interference in their spiritual liberties.

It was also during the nineteenth century that 'liberal' theology (p. 9) from Germany came to have a great influence in Scotland. To a large extent this happened because it was felt that ministers ought to be much better educated than they had been, and many were sent to Germany to study.

The Presbyterian system

The word 'presbyter' is from a Greek word *presbuteros*, usually translated 'elder' in the New Testament. It is generally recognized that in the early church, elders (the name for the office) did the actual work of a bishop, which literally means 'an overseer'. So elders are fundamental to the whole system. Ministers are simply one kind of elder. The distinction is usually made between preaching elders (ministers) and ruling elders (lay people who share in the running of the parish). But both have the same authority. Both are ordained and elected for life, unless they resign or are deposed.

The system of church government revolves round four councils or 'courts', each court having authority over those below it, except in certain circumstances.

At the parish level, responsibility is in the hands of the Kirk Session, ministers and elders together. Elders assist the minister, for example in the Communion service, in admitting and caring for new members, and in pastoral visitation. An elder may be responsible for, say, twenty members. deacons (or managers) have responsibility for the church buildings and for some financial matters.

The Presbytery is in many ways the most influential court. It is a meeting of all the ministers and an equal number of elders from churches in the area (which, of course, may vary in size). It exercises a fair degree of control and supervision over the churches, and acts as an appeal court for decisions of the Kirk Session. Ministers are not members of the local church, but of the Presbytery, which supervises their appointment. Members of the local church nominate new ministers, but they must be approved by the Presbytery, to whom they are responsible, and who alone can remove them.

The next court is the annual Synod, consisting of representatives from the Presbyteries. From the Synod, representatives are elected to the highest authority of the Church, the General Assembly. It meets annually, with an equal number of ministers and elders. Whatever decisions are made, they are binding on all the churches.

The teaching

All Presbyterian churches officially acknowledge the Bible to be the Word of God, the supreme authority for faith and life. But a subordinate standard has always been the Westminster Confession of Faith (1646) with its 33 chapters, and the Longer and Shorter Catechisms of the Westminster Assembly (1643–9). Many churches and ministers believe that the Confession is as relevant today as ever. Others interpret it liberally, feeling it is of only limited value.

The doctrines at its heart are usually termed Calvinistic (or Reformed) (p. 11). They include: the sovereignty of God, election, predestination and 'the final perseverance of the saints' (that once people are born again, they cannot lose their salvation); Jesus Christ is the head of the Church, the only mediator between God and man, and he rules in his Church. Stress is also laid on the identification of the

Jewish Sabbath and the Christian Sunday, and the need to observe the Sabbath rest.

These are some of its declarations:

> God from all eternity did, by the most wise and holy counsel of his own will, freely and unchangeably ordain whatever comes to pass. Yet . . . neither is God the author of sin nor is violence offered to the will of the creatures . . . By the decree of God, for the manifestation of His glory, some men and angels are predestinated to everlasting life, and others fore-ordained to everlasting death. They whom God hath accepted . . . can neither totally nor finally fall away from the state of grace; but shall certainly persevere therein to the end and be eternally saved. The . . . universal Church, which is invisible, consists of the whole number of the elect. The visible Church . . . consists of all those throughout the world that profess the true religion, together with their children.

The Church of Scotland

It is often known simply as 'the Kirk', and has about 675,000 members. In Scotland, it is the 'established' Church, the national Church. But it is free from state interference. It is able to make its own appointments. A representative of the sovereign is invited to the General Assembly, but only as an observer. The members of the Royal Family go to the Church of Scotland when they are north of the border. Being established means that the Church feels its responsibility for the community as a whole. This can be seen especially when large-scale disasters take place.

The Church's Constitution declares their worship of the Trinity, and their proclamation of the forgiveness of sins and acceptance with God through faith in Christ, with the gift of eternal life. Although most of the ministers and members see themselves as having a simple loyalty to the Church as such, differences in theology are apparent. Every minister and elder (who can be men or women) must give assent to the Westminster Confession when they are ordained. But many liberals (p. 9) feel it has little use today, and cannot accept much of the Bible's teaching, wanting to explore new ways of thinking. On the other hand, 'evangelicals' (p. 10) accept the authority of the Bible as it is, proclaiming its teaching and that of the Westminster Confession. In recent years, it seems that evangelicals have been growing in numbers. Some estimates suggest that a quarter to a third of all ministers are now evangelical, some say even more.

Worship is usually simple and dignified. It includes hymns and metrical psalms, with prayers and Bible readings, led by the minister, who wears a gown and preaching bands. An increasing number of churches include modern 'spiritual songs'. Because the sermon has always been of greatest importance, the pulpit is central in the building. Sermons may be half or three-quarters of an hour in length. But not always!

Certain churches are more 'high' than others, using a liturgy with printed responses, and emphasising the sacraments.

It may be because emotion has been played down, that the charismatic renewal (p. 16) has not made much impact in the Church. Nevertheless there are some 'charismatic' churches with free prayer and the gifts of the Spirit being encouraged. A renewal group is emerging, with a network of prayer.

Baptism is for infants, 'as a sign and seal of the covenant of grace', and is taken by the minister. The parents must be at least adherents of the church, who will undertake to give the child a Christian upbringing. Those who have been baptised as infants cannot be baptised again as adults.

Communion, the Lord's Supper, is a solemn occasion. Because of its seriousness, it is usually celebrated only once every three months, although some churches have it halfyearly, others monthly, a few weekly. The table is open to Christians from other churches. The old practice of 'fencing the Table' is still observed by some, more so in country areas. A day or two before the Communion service, sermons are preached, pointing out the solemn responsibility of examining one's life before taking the bread and wine.

Remarriage is possible after divorce, but ministers must investigate and make up their own minds about each situation.

The General Assembly has shown its disapproval of abortion and gambling, declaring its hostility to the National Lottery. Homosexual practice has been frowned upon, but the debate is continuing.

The Church has led the way in educational and social reforms. It is largely because of the Church's influence that the Scottish education system is acknowledged as better than most. The Church's Board of Social Responsibility is the largest voluntary social services organisation in Scotland. It has a vast range of facilities, e.g. day centres, homes for the elderly, nurseries, food clubs, credit unions, hostels for the homeless, counselling centres, care for AIDS sufferers, alcoholics, drug addicts, the mentally ill and those with learning disabilities.

Missionaries overseas work mainly in parts of Africa and the Caribbean. The Church is involved with the ecumenical movement (p. 15).

The Free Church of Scotland

In 1900, a union took place between the Free Church and the United Presbyterian Church, to form the United Free

Church. But a minority did not agree to the union, and continued as the Free Church, often known as the 'Wee Frees'. They wanted to keep an unmodified Westminster Confession. In worship, only metrical psalms are sung without musical accompaniment. Women cannot be ministers. The Church is strongest in north and northwest Scotland, the Highlands and Islands, with some 19,000 members.

The United Free Church of Scotland

In 1929, a union took place between the United Free Church and the Church of Scotland. But a minority did not agree to that union, and continued as the United Free Church. They believed it was wrong to have a formal connection with the state, because it could so easily interfere with spiritual freedom. A distinctive feature is that lay people can become moderators (chairmen) of Presbyteries and the General Assembly. Women can be ordained to the ministry and eldership. Members of other churches are welcome to Communion. The Church is involved with Action Together of Churches in Scotland (ACTS) and the ecumenical movement generally.

The Church believes it has the right to modify the Westminster Confession, if they feel it necessary. It has some 7000 members.

The Free Presbyterian Church of Scotland

Founded in 1893 as a breakaway from the Free Church of Scotland, it has an uncompromising commitment to Calvinism (p. 11). Having 4000 members, their strongest area is the Western Isles. No instrumental music is used in worship. For them, 'the Book of Psalms is the divinely appointed manual of praise'. Sunday (the Sabbath) must be kept strictly, and members should not smoke, drink, dance or gamble.

Associated Presbyterian Churches of Scotland

Formed in 1989 as a breakaway from the Free Presbyterians, they felt that certain principles like liberty of conscience and the communion of saints were not being upheld. In worship, psalms are sung unaccompanied. Membership is something over a thousand.

The Presbyterian Church in Ireland

The largest Presbyterian Church in the Province, it has 194,000 members, and is very similar to the Church of Scotland. The first Presbytery was formed in 1642. But it was only in 1840 that two Synods united to form the General Assembly of the Presbyterian Church in Ireland. Liberty of interpretation is allowed about some parts of the Westminster Confession. Women can be ministers and elders.

Worship is dignified, usually consisting of hymns, metrical psalms, prayers, with the sermon looked upon as highly important. The charismatic (p. 16) renewal has had very little impact. The Church is in the forefront of ecumenical activity (p. 15) in Ireland.

Social work is extensive — homes for the elderly, help for young offenders, alcoholics, drug addicts, AIDS victims, etc. They also run a special Church for the Deaf.

Missionaries work in India, Nepal, Indonesia, Africa, Jamaica.

The Free Presbyterian Church of Ulster

Formed in 1951 through Dr Ian Paisley and having over 14,000 members, they maintain a strict Calvinistic (p. 11) theology. The highest court of the Church is the Presbytery, which meets every month and consists of ministers and elders of the churches. The communicant members of each church elect their own ministers and elders.

Members can decide for themselves which kind of baptism to adopt. No one method is laid down. The Lord's Supper is usually held monthly.

Seven independent Christian day schools are run by the churches.

Non-subscribing Presbyterian Church of Ireland

The name comes from the fact that they do not 'subscribe' to the Westminster Confession, i.e. they do not hold to it as their confession of faith. In fact, no particular creed or confession is acknowledged. The Bible, which is seen as the only basis of faith, must be applied by each person individually.

Often thought of as Unitarian, there are links with the Unitarian Church in England. But they say they are not Unitarian as such (Unitarians deny the Trinity, saying there is only one Person in the Godhead). In fact, some members may be Unitarian, but no theology is laid down to which all must assent.

Separating from the Irish Presbyterian Church in the 1720s and also in the 1820s, their organisation is on the usual Presbyterian lines. Baptism is for all children whose parents desire it. The Communion service is open to all. Ministers, who may be men or women, are allowed to marry divorced people. The Church is committed to the ecumenical movement (p. 15). Having about 3500 members, nearly all the churches are in Northern Ireland.

The Presbyterian Church of Wales

The Methodist Revival in Wales in the mid-eighteenth century was largely due to the preaching of men like Griffith Jones, Howell Harris and Daniel Rowlands. Others who had a great influence were George Whitefield and William Williams, the hymnwriter. Each of them was Calvinistic (p. 11) in theology. An 'Association of Calvinistic Methodists' was first held in 1743. Continuing to meet together, they nevertheless remained in the Anglican Church until 1811, when they became independent.

A Confession of Faith was published in 1823, based on the Thirty-nine Articles of the Church of England and the Westminster Confession. The first General Assembly was held in 1864 in Swansea.

They are now called The Presbyterian Church of Wales, with the alternative title of The Calvinistic Methodist Church of Wales. This latter title distinguishes them from the (English) Methodists, whose theology is Arminian (p. 11). In fact nowadays, the preaching is not necessarily Calvinistic, and a variety of theological positions is found in the denomination.

The organisation is basically Presbyterian, but the Church has three provinces: an Association in the South, one in the North and one in the East. Being members of the Churches Together in Wales, discussions have been held with other denominations to try to form a United Free Church in Wales.

The Church has shown a keen interest in education, politics and social work. They have strongly denounced the National Lottery. The membership is about 50,000.

Quakers or Society of Friends

The Society of Friends, or Quakers as they are most often called, were founded by George Fox (1624–91). He did not originally see himself as the founder of a sect, but as an evangelist. He came from a godly Puritan home, and was a weaver by trade. As a child, he saw that churchgoers professed a great deal, but often did not lead a truly Christian life. Integrity to him was essential. People needed to have a first-hand experience of Christ. He felt he had to draw them away from what he saw as only 'religion', from ceremonies and merely human ideas.

He met a group of people who had already left the churches, calling themselves 'seekers' and waiting in silence for God to speak to them. He became their leader. Gradually a simple organisation came into being.

Fox became known for his outspokenness, often interrupting church services. For this and other acts of 'rebellion', he was imprisoned eight times in six years. The name 'Quakers' was given to them by a judge because, in 1650, George Fox told him to 'tremble at the Word of the Lord'. The name has also been used to describe the emotion often shown in their meetings. Since the early nineteenth century, they have called themselves 'The Society of Friends'.

Fox believed that Christianity should not be tied down to a theology, or have a great church organisation, with clergy. He insisted that outward belief did not bring salvation. Creeds had been formulated by fallible human beings, and cannot define religious experience. The visible church had departed from its New Testament roots. Now Christ was going to gather the true church.

He said, 'every man was enlightened by the Divine Light of Christ'. He encouraged his followers to meet together in silence to wait before God and listen for his voice. 'Truth cannot be confined within a Creed. We commit ourselves not to words, but to a way. We have found corporately that the Spirit, if rightly followed, will lead into truth, unity and love.' Quakers were to dress very simply, not to take part in war, not to swear an oath, but to be very much concerned about others' social needs. They were to work hard and, having prospered, would be able to give generously to needy people.

Quaker theology, such as it was, was put in a systematic form by Robert Barclay in his book, *Apology for The True Christian Divinity* (1678).

In the early days, Quakers had to endure great persecution, to some extent because of their open criticism of the churches. But it was also because they did not take oaths in court or take off their hats in the presence of magistrates. During the reign of Charles II, 12,000 were put in prison, and over 300 died there. Even so, numbers grew and, by 1700, membership was about 60,000, the highest number recorded.

The movement started in the north of England, but gradually moved south, and then into Europe and North America. They have always challenged the conventions of the day in politics, in business, in the law, in the established church, in social etiquette and in education. They have worked for improvement in prisons (e.g. Elizabeth Fry), the abolition of the slave trade, and the emancipation of women. They have won renown for public schools they founded, and also for institutions for the mentally ill. They have fought against poverty and against injustice, especially for those imprisoned for religious, political or other beliefs. William Penn founded Pennsylvania in the USA on Quaker principles. Cadbury, Rowntree and Fry set up their model factories, caring for their workers in a new way.

The inward light

It is their conviction that the 'inward light' coming from God is of greater authority than the Bible. The Bible is a faithful historical account of what has happened in the past, and of what has been believed. But it is not infallible for today, and can only have a secondary role. Because of this, Quakers do not always hold to what other Christians would see as basic teaching. A place must be given to people with different theologies. So for instance, there are Quakers who are universalist, saying that ultimately everybody will be in heaven. Others are definitely evangelical (p. 10). The range is wide.

It is maintained that creeds are not necessarily wrong, but they can only be provisional not ultimate truth. Room must be made for development and progress. Belief is too deep to be contained in propositions. It is shown in action. Criticism has been levelled at them because, with no clear-cut theology, it may not be possible for them to help those who are searching for the truth. Their answer is that God works directly in the soul, uniting people to Christ, and enabling them to live in a simple, pure and truthful way.

Simplicity is at the heart of all Quaker ethics – no excesses of dress, behaviour or possessions – an emphasis on moderation, honesty, integrity. They are encouraged to listen to each other in humility and understanding, trusting in the

Spirit. It is important to be honest with oneself, and face shortcomings, receiving ministry from others in the right spirit.

The meeting-houses are very simple, with benches or chairs round the four walls. They meet together in silence, but anyone, man or woman, can pray or speak as they are moved by the Spirit. No-one leads and everyone should be ready to participate. It is important to prepare beforehand in heart and mind. But 'we need to find a way into silence which allows us to deepen our awareness of the divine and to find the inward source of our strength'. The meetings are brought to a close by the elders shaking hands.

Baptism or Communion services are not held, because they are interpreted in spiritual terms. These are not wrong, they say, but are not essential. The outward symbol is less important than the inward life of the spirit.

In a few 'meetings', a Bible study is held, and 'spiritual songs' are sung.

Their organisation

Quakers have no ordained ministry, but have officers, men or women, with certain responsibilities. 'Elders' arrange the meetings, and see they are properly run. 'Overseers' help in giving pastoral care.

'Monthly Meetings' are the chief meetings for church affairs. Votes are not taken, because that would emphasise division. It is a 'sense of meeting' that is important. If necessary, a decision will be postponed until there is unity. 'Think it possible that you may be mistaken.'

Gatherings of representatives are held at local, area, regional and national level. The Britain Yearly Meeting (previously called the London Yearly Meeting) is the main authority for England, Scotland and Wales. Worldwide, there are over 50 autonomous Yearly Meetings, and a total membership of some 200,000. In Britain, membership is over 18,000, which includes children.

Their influence

Nowadays, the belief is no longer held that Quakerism is the only true church. In fact, they are active in many ecumenical (p. 15) projects. This is despite the fact that they are not members of the World Council of Churches, not being able to accept the credal basis. Observers are sent to the meetings. But they are in membership with the Council of Churches in Britain and Ireland, and the Churches Together in England, Scotland and Wales, where there is not the same credal basis.

Although a wide variety of conviction and practice exists in other ways, the conviction would seem to be unanimous that they should not participate in war. War and preparation for war are inconsistent with the spirit of Christ. As well as this, oaths are never taken in court, because to do so implies a double standard of truth. Their word should be accepted. They 'affirm', but do not 'swear'.

Quakers are still in the forefront of humanitarian action throughout the world and in working for peace, having an influence out of all proportion to their numbers. Deep concern is continually being voiced about the trade in weapons and nuclear proliferation, as well as the problems of race and those posed by new technologies, e.g. genetic engineering.

Roman Catholic Church

The Roman Catholic Church is by far the largest Christian denomination in the world. Its community (those who would call themselves Catholic) is about 900 million, round about half of the worldwide Christian community. The Church has had a massive influence on world history.

It sees itself as having unbroken links with the apostolic church, i.e. the church of the New Testament. Active in almost every country, it is particularly strong in Italy, Spain, Portugal, Central and South America. The word 'Catholic' means universal, worldwide. But the Church is 'Roman' in the sense that its headquarters is at the Vatican, situated in Rome.

In AD 451, the Council of Chalcedon took place with representatives from almost every part of the world where Christian churches existed at that time. This 'Ecumenical Council' decided that the Bishop of Rome, Leo the Great and all his successors, should be called Pope, 'father'. Leo himself claimed he should be recognised as the Universal Bishop, i.e. over every part of the Church. However, the Church in the East of the Roman Empire, based on Constantinople (now Istanbul), did not accept his authority.

Gradually the gap widened between West and East. Finally, the Pope excommunicated the Church in the East, the Orthodox Church. In the West, the power of the Pope increased until it was claimed he could give or take empires and kingdoms, and that every human being should be subject to him.

Nobody knows precisely how Christianity was brought to Britain in the first place. It may have been through Roman soldiers and traders. We do know that in the fifth to the seventh centuries, Patrick was active in Ireland, Columba in Scotland, David in Wales, Cuthbert and Aidan in England, as well as many others. By the time Pope Gregory sent Augustine to Britain in 597, Christian churches were widespread. But their 'Celtic' kind of Christianity was not the same as the 'Roman' kind. In 664 at the Synod of Whitby, their respective merits were discussed. Rome triumphed and, in effect, ruled until the Reformation, when the Church of England was founded in 1534.

After the Reformation, the fortunes of the Catholic Church in the British Isles fluctuated. They made little headway, except in Ireland, until certain restrictions were taken away in the early nineteenth century. They then began to flourish in England, partly because of the many Irish immigrants who came across as a result of the potato famines. A boost was also given when John Henry Newman, a leading Anglican, became a Roman Catholic in 1845, and was made a Cardinal.

In Ireland, apart from the North where many Presbyterian Scots were encouraged to settle when James I was king, the Reformation hardly made any impression at all, perhaps because it was associated with England. At the same time, Catholicism has never made great headway in Wales.

The Mass attendance figures are approximately: England, slightly over a million; Wales, 47,000; Scotland, 250,000; N. Ireland, 500,000.

The Second Vatican Council

Following the Reformation, great numbers left the Catholic Church to join the Protestant churches. Pope Paul III decided to launch the Counter-Reformation, and summoned the Council of Trent (1545–63). The Council came out strongly against Protestantism, although denouncing a number of evils and corruptions in the Church itself. It also reaffirmed and clarified many of the Church's doctrines, e.g. the importance of the seven sacraments for salvation, that the Church has the sole right to interpret the Bible, the celibacy of the clergy, and the existence of Purgatory.

The decisions of the Council underpinned the whole outlook of the Church until Pope John XXIII called the Second Vatican Council (1962–5). He said it was needed 'to update the Church'. Nearly 2500 bishops thoroughly examined every aspect of the Church's life and teaching; also its relationships with other churches and with society generally. It came up with some far-reaching decisions, which many welcomed, although not everybody. Since then, changes have taken place which some have resisted, whilst others have wished they had been taken much further.

The main decisions (more detail under particular headings) were concerning worship, e.g. an encouragement to use a country's own language instead of Latin, the Bible and preaching were to be given a more prominent place, and lay people were to play a greater part in the conduct of worship and in pastoral ministry.

One of the more important decisions was to make a change in attitude towards other churches. Protestants were no longer to be called 'heretics', but 'separated brethren'. Other churches were to be recognised as such, and theological discussions have since been taking place with some of them, e.g. ARCIC (Anglican-Roman Catholic International Convention). Collaboration on social and humanitarian action has been increasing.

Although now conceding that Christian life and truth are not limited only to the Catholic Church, they have no doubt it is there that these are most clearly found. The 'fulness of the means of salvation' can only be found in the Catholic Church. But those who believe in Christ and have undergone a legitimate baptism have a certain, if imperfect, communion with the Church. The relationship with the Orthodox Church is such that it is permissible to celebrate the Eucharist together. This does not apply to other churches.

The Catholic Church is involved with the 'Churches Together' in each of the four UK countries. It is not a member of the World Council of Churches, although 'observers' are sent to the meetings.

The authority of the hierarchy

This is seen as vital for the whole life of the Church. Christ has given authority to the Pope, the bishops and the priests. The pope is Christ's representative on earth, 'the Vicar of Christ'. It is believed that he is the successor to Peter as the Bishop of Rome, and that Peter passed on his authority to his successors for all time.

The bishops are seen as the true successors of the Apostles. The phrase 'apostolic succession' means that each bishop is consecrated by other bishops, with the line of consecration going back to the Apostles. Just as the Apostles were given authority to baptise, teach and forgive, so the bishops have the same authority. It is they who bring unity to the Church, with the Pope being the centre of that unity.

The Pope is the head of a 'college of bishops', where all are equal. He is elected by the cardinals, who are senior bishops, themselves appointed by a Pope. The election of a Pope is now by secret ballot.

Since Vatican II, the Pope cannot exercise authority by himself. The Pope and bishops together lay down the teaching for the whole Church. They have confidence in the full inspiration and authority of the Bible, although for them it includes the Apocrypha (twelve books which were in the Greek translation of the Old Testament, but were not in the Hebrew Bible). But it is the Church (through the Pope and bishops) who alone can interpret the Bible rightly, for the Church gave birth to Scripture, and through tradition has been interpreting the Bible for 2000 years. It was the Church that formulated the Apostles' and Nicene creeds.

Their criticism of Protestants is that they allow too much individuality in biblical understanding. At the same time, Protestants have accused Catholics of allowing tradition (the accumulated teaching) to be more important than the Bible. In reply to that, Catholics would say that God has protected the Church from teaching error, and that when pronouncements are made about beliefs or morals the teaching is infallible. One aspect of faith is to accept all that God reveals through the Church as it makes biblical revelation authentic for each generation. However, many Catholics today find it difficult to accept some of the teaching (details later).

The bishops meet regularly for consultation. Every country or region has its Bishops' Conference. Representatives from these meet in Rome every two or three years to discuss issues of the day.

Countries are divided into provinces under an archbishop. Under them are bishops, responsible for a diocese.

In the UK, the provinces are Westminster, Liverpool, Birmingham, Southwark, Cardiff, Glasgow, St Andrews, Edinburgh and Armagh.

At parish level, the priest is central. The whole concept of a priest is that he is some kind of a mediator between people and God. In the Catholic Church, he has always had great authority. At his ordination, he is authorised to represent the whole Church, and therefore Christ himself. This authority is particularly seen in the sacraments, whose effectiveness is dependent on him.

Nevertheless, since Vatican II, a priest is looked upon, not so much as a man with power, but as a man of service. It is now stated that, although all Christians are priests (as Protestants believe), the ministerial priests are there to serve the ordinary priests. One result of this is that more instruction is now given to candidates before baptism, confirmation, confession and marriage, because it is important that these sacraments are not only received, but received in the right spirit.

A parish may have more than one priest. Only men can be priests, and they cannot be married, although much debate is taking place as to whether it is necessary for them to be celibate.

A deacon may help the priests. He is ordained, but does not have the same authority as a priest. He can be married. He may assist in preaching, in funerals, in marriage, etc.

Lay people now help much more in the decision-making of parish councils. Some are parish administrators or parish counsellors. They may help the priest in the services and even take communion to sick people. Many teach the faith in schools, universities and seminaries, where only priests taught before.

The seven sacraments

These are at the heart of the Church. It is believed that the grace of God is conferred on those receiving them. Christ himself is there and is active. This is guaranteed by the ordained priesthood. The sacraments are essential for salvation and for every part of the Christian life. They confer grace, not because of the righteousness of the priest (or bishop) or of those receiving them, but simply because of the power of Christ.

1. Baptism

This is the basis of the Christian life. Baptism is administered by the priest with holy (specially blessed) water. This may be by immersion or by pouring the water over the head. It is accompanied by the sign of the cross, the word being proclaimed, exorcism, and anointing with oil. The infant (as it usually is, but it could be an older person) is then pronounced clear of original sin (sin which is inherited) and all past sins; he or she has been reborn as a child of God and has become a member of the body of Christ, the Church. Baptism gives access to the other sacraments. It cannot be repeated.

If a child dies before being baptised, the Church does not say definitely what happens to them. Some theologians teach that an unbaptised baby goes straight to heaven. Some maintain the older view, that they go to limbo, a place which does not involve either the sufferings of hell or the blessings of heaven.

2. Confirmation

At this sacrament, the grace of God is received in a further way by those who have already received it in baptism. It usually takes place after the seventh birthday. Some are admitted to their First Communion at that age.

The baptismal promises and confession of faith are renewed. The bishop then anoints with oil (chrism) and says, 'Be sealed with the gift of the Holy Spirit'. Those confirmed in this way are more perfectly bound to the Church.

All members of the Church have certain obligations. The minimum is:

(a) to attend Mass on Sundays and holy days;
(b) to confess their sins at least once a year;
(c) to attend Mass during the Easter season;
(d) to observe the stated fast days;
(e) to give to the Church as they are able.

Members must not be involved with spiritism or fortune-telling, nor become Freemasons.

3. Eucharist (Mass)

Eucharist means 'thanksgiving'. This is the very centre of church life. As well as the actual Communion, the service includes readings from the Bible, prayers, reciting the Nicene Creed and a 'homily', a sermon. Lay people usually take part.

When the priest repeats the words of Christ at the Last Supper, the bread and wine are consecrated by the Holy Spirit. It is said that, although they still appear to be bread and wine, they have now become the body and blood of Christ. The process is called 'transubstantiation'.

Today it is emphasised that the sacrifice of Christ is not repeated. It is celebrated. When Jesus died on the cross, it was a once-for-all sacrifice for the sins of men and women. Now, as that sacrifice is recalled and proclaimed, it is made effective here and now. It is re-presented. Christ offers himself as the true food and drink.

The congregation come forward to receive both bread and wine. This is now the norm. (Before, they could only receive the bread.) But they must prepare so as to be worthy to receive Christ.

Christians from other churches cannot receive the communion (except those from the Orthodox Church). The belief is that communion with Christ at the Eucharist cannot be separated from union with him in the faith of the Catholic Church.

Elements from the Communion are 'reserved' in a tabernacle, so that they can be taken immediately to a seriously ill person, in addition to being a source of devotion.

4. Penance and reconciliation (popularly called confession)

At baptism, a freeing from original sin takes place. But the sacrament of penance is when a serious sin has taken place after baptism.

The Church believes there are two kinds of sin, 'mortal' and 'venial'. Mortal sins are often described as 'grave' sins, those which destroy friendship with God, e.g. idolatry, murder, adultery, perjury, oppression of the poor, blasphemy. A deliberate choice of evil has been made. 'Venial' sins are lesser sins like envy, anger, lust, greed, idleness. By themselves, they do not break the covenant with God. But they need to be confessed regularly, even if not to a priest. Provision is made in the Eucharist for this. Repentance is necessary, which should lead to acts of love towards others.

However, when a mortal sin has been committed, it is necessary, not only to repent, but to seek reconciliation with God and the Church through the sacrament of penance. It must certainly be done before taking Communion. Confession of any mortal sin must be made to the priest, who is able to give 'absolution'. In the absolution, the priest will include the words, 'Through the ministry of the Church, may God give you pardon and peace, and I absolve you from your sins, in the name of the Father, and of the Son, and of the Holy Spirit'.

Protestants question why the confession should be to the priest, and not simply to God. The Catholic Church states that, because of his ordination, the priest speaks in the name of the whole Church, and therefore in the name of Christ himself. Mortal sins can lead to hell and eternal punishment. So it is important that assurance is received that the sins have been forgiven by God. Jesus gave to Peter and the Apostles the authority to bind and loose.

A symbolic penance will also be given, perhaps involving acts of self-denial, helping others, prayer, an offering, and especially repairing any harm that has been done.

The teaching about purgatory: although reconciliation takes place through the sacrament, it is said that every sin, even a venial sin, affects the sinner in some way. This means that, after death, a purifying is still needed. This takes place in purgatory, where punishment is given and holiness is achieved, thus allowing entrance into heaven.

For those in purgatory, prayers can be made, so that they may be more quickly loosed from their sins. At the same time, they can be helped by the prayers and the 'treasury' of good works of Mary and the saints. This treasury or reservoir of merit is more than the saints need for themselves. They can pass this extra merit on to those who need it and ask for it. The saints are those whom the Church holds up as examples of holy living. They are 'canonised', declared to be a saint after a long process of investigation.

5. *The anointing of the sick*

This used to be called 'extreme unction', and was usually given when somebody was dying. Since Vatican II, it has been used in a more general way. Sometimes it is given at the Eucharist, but it can be given at any time when somebody is seriously ill. The priest anoints the forehead and hands with oil, and prays.

6. Ordination

It is through being ordained that a priest is given the authority to represent Christ in the Church, especially in the sacraments. As was said earlier, he must be male and not married. The bishop lays his hands on the candidate, speaks the words of consecration, and in this way the Holy Spirit is given to him for his particular responsibilities. Now, any sin committed by the priest cannot stop the grace of God coming through the sacraments.

In the ordination of a bishop, several other bishops take part.

7. Marriage (matrimony)

Through this sacrament, the man and the woman, united by the priest, are given grace to grow in love and face problems together. In these days, it is emphasised that they are making a covenant. In other words, they have their responsibilities as well.

A marriage is expected to be permanent. Even if a civil divorce takes place, the marriage is still valid in the eyes of the Church. If it has been consummated, it can only be dissolved by death. Remarriage after a civil divorce is counted as adultery, and therefore is a mortal sin. Those remarried cannot receive Communion.

Marriages can be annulled. This means that the Church pronounces that what was thought to be a marriage never in fact properly existed for one reason or another.

When marriages are 'mixed', i.e. one of the partners is not a Catholic, they need to be given special dispensation. The Catholic partner must be ready to take responsibility for the children's education as Catholics.

Although the Church used to say that the purpose of sex in marriage was simply that children might be born, now it is recognised that sexual love is on a par with procreation. Nevertheless, artificial contraception is forbidden. The only method of contraception authorised is the 'rhythm' method, when sex takes place during the monthly infertile periods. In fact, it seems that today most Catholics decide for themselves, maintaining they are not being responsible parents if they do not use artificial means.

Abortion is a mortal sin, and so is any kind of co-operation with it. The Church says that life begins at the moment of conception. Therefore abortion is murder. Many take the view that a possible exception is when the mother's life is in danger.

Official teaching is also that the Church is opposed to *in vitro* fertilisation, and all research involving embryos.

Homosexual acts are condemned.

The place of Mary

Mary, the mother of Jesus, is the first of the saints and the model of faith and discipleship. Because she accepted her role as the mother of Jesus, she helped to bring salvation to the world. Without her faithfulness, Christ would not have been given to the world.

Catholics have often seen her as a sympathetic figure who could mediate between the believer and Christ. It is hardly possible to draw near to the Son except through his mother. She is called Advocate, Helper, Benefactress and

Mediatrix. However, Vatican II made it clear that this does not take away or add anything 'to the dignity and efficacy of Christ, the one mediator'.

The devotion which is given to her is not the same quality of worship that is given to God. This applies to all the saints. However, it is possible to pray to her, e.g. in this way: 'Hail Mary, full of grace . . . mother of God, pray for us sinners now and at the hour of our death'.

The doctrine of the Immaculate Conception was issued in 1854. This stated that from the first moment of her conception, she was entirely free from original sin. Thus she is a symbol of freedom from sin, which would eventually come to all believers in heaven.

The doctrine of the Assumption, defined in 1950, states that Mary was taken up both body and soul into heaven, there to reign as Queen of Heaven. In this way, she is seen as a symbol of resurrection.

Many Protestants find that the place Catholics give to Mary is a particularly difficult area of disagreement, because it goes beyond the Bible description of her.

Religious orders

Down the years, the monastic and other 'orders' have been very influential in the life of the Church. For instance, the Benedictines, founded in the sixth century, have had a monastic rule which is still the basis of monasticism. They concentrate on contemplation, and on cultural and educational work. The Dominicans, founded in the thirteenth century, specialize in preaching and theological study. The Jesuits have had the greatest influence. Founded in the sixteenth century by Ignatious Loyola, they take not only the usual vows of poverty, chastity and obedience, but also one of complete loyalty to the Pope, ready to do immediately whatever he might wish, especially with a view to gaining converts.

Today, in a variety of orders, men (both ordained and lay) and women run monasteries, convents, schools, retreat houses, homes for the elderly, etc. as well as taking part in worship and prayer, they can be involved with all kinds of social and humanitarian work.

The Catholic charismatic renewal

The initial spark came in 1967 when a group of Catholics met in Duquesne University, USA, and were baptised in the Spirit simultaneously. Since then, it has spread to most areas of the Catholic world (p. 16). Perhaps the most influential leader was Cardinal Suenens of Belgium. In 1975, he was authorised by Pope Paul VI to oversee the development of the renewal.

In 1993, a Decree was issued by the Vatican which recognised the International Catholic Charismatic Renewal Services as an official body for the promotion of the renewal throughout the world.

Some estimates suggest that nearly 10% of Catholics have been affected through the renewal, perhaps 90 million. All parts of the Church in the British Isles have their own renewal organisation. Conferences are held. Prayer and healing centres have been opened. Some people have decided to live in community, and have been able to help alcoholics and drug addicts.

It is recognised that without Vatican II, the renewal would probably not have happened. Possibly the most important factor has been the encouragement to read and study the Bible. Bible study groups have proliferated.

Leaders of the renewal maintain that the baptism in the Spirit, coming after repentance, revitalises the previous water baptism. Jesus becomes real as never before, and changes lives. The Eucharist takes on new meaning. The gifts of the Spirit have brought new life to many local churches.

Relationships with Christians in other denominations have been a feature of the renewal. Occasionally, joint conferences are held.

Not all in the Church have welcomed the renewal. Some have opposed it. But the renewal leaders believe it is going to spread further.

Tensions within the Church

It is important to distinguish between the official teaching of the Church, and the way Catholics react to the teaching. Because of the new openness since Vatican II, people feel much more free to disagree. Schools of theology have sometimes come up with radical views, and some theologians have been disciplined for going too far. Although it has always been said that faith means accepting the teaching of the Church, many would dispute that today.

To some extent, this new attitude has been fuelled by the fact that the number of priests has continued to fall and the number of lapsed Catholics has continued to rise. A well-known statistic is that, since 1980, about 50,000 Catholics have lapsed — they no longer attend Mass — in the Archdiocese of Liverpool. Not everybody agrees about the reason. Some say it is because of all the changes that have taken place. Others say it is because not enough changes have taken place. So there are two main camps, the 'traditionalists' and the 'progressives'.

The traditionalists

These are sure that Christ founded the Catholic Church to preserve and teach his message, and there is no other church that can do that. Many are opposed to Vatican II. Certainly, the Church has gone too far too quickly. They feel betrayed because it is not the Catholic Church they used to know, and say the bishops do not give a strong enough lead on real Catholic teaching.

At one extreme, there are those who feel that only the Latin Mass authorised by the Council of Trent is faithful to the traditions of the Church. But most traditionalists would say that some recent trends need to be reversed, e.g. aspects of the liturgy, lay participation, closer ties with other churches, and where any slackening of teaching on social matters has taken place. The authority of the Church needs to be restored.

The progressives

These feel that many more changes are needed, both in doctrine and in practice. Some are moving in an evangelical direction (p. 10). An Evangelical Catholic Movement has its supporters, loyal to Rome, but subscribing to a statement of evangelical beliefs, including justification by faith. Others could be termed 'liberal' (p. 9), believing that people today will not put up with some of the 'conservative' pronouncements of the Church, especially on social issues.

Here are some of the issues which are causing vigorous debate in the Church:

(1) More *lay involvement*, e.g. in decision-making, in the sacraments, even the right to preside at the Eucharist. Some want the priests simply to be team leaders, saying this would help to mitigate the priest shortage.

(2) *Celibacy of the priesthood*. A sensitive issue today because of sexual scandals and because married priests have come over from the Church of England. It is said that celibacy is the chief reason why priests resign. Opinion seems to be growing that priests should be allowed to marry.

(3) *Ordination of women*. Not yet very widespread, but the feminist movement and the need for more priests are making some feel it should be looked into.

(4) *Artificial contraception*. This is taking place widely in any case, and so, it is said, it should be allowed officially; also because of the world's population increase and the spread of AIDS.

(5) *Abortion*. This has widespread support, that the Church's rigid teaching should be changed.

(6) *Divorce*. Those remarried after divorce should be admitted to the sacraments.

(7) *Homosexual practice*. Not perhaps a widely held view, but some writers say this ought to be allowed, and that same-sex unions should be blessed by the Church.

(8) The doctrines of the *infallibility* of Vatican pronouncements, the sinlessness and bodily assumption of Mary. Certain theologians continually question these doctrines.

Most of these reforms are supported by a British organisation called 'Catholics for a Changing Church', who are 'for progress in the spirit of Vatican II' believing the Church is too centralised, too hierarchical, and out of touch with present-day values. Greater freedom should be allowed about theological matters. They want power to be transferred from Rome to a national synod of bishops. Decision-making should be only after widespread consultation.

Salvation Army

William Booth (1829–1912) and his wife, Catherine, founded the East London Christian Mission in 1865. William had been a Methodist minister and a very effective evangelist. He began the Mission because he was afraid that his converts would find it difficult to settle in the usual churches. Immediately, there was outstanding success as more and more mission halls were opened in London's East End.

In 1878, he announced a new organisation, which would be 'a Salvation Army to carry the blood of Christ and the power of the Holy Ghost to every corner of the world'. (The Army motto is still 'Blood and Fire', the blood of Christ and the fire of the Holy Spirit.)

Military language took over, reflecting the spiritual warfare in which they were engaging. William Booth became 'the General', in complete charge of the work. He was even able to nominate his successor, and his own son, William Bramwell Booth, became the General in 1912. Mission stations became 'corps'; military titles were used throughout and uniforms worn.

Booth's great ambition was to reach poor and downtrodden people. By 1884, 900 corps had been established. This was in spite of much opposition, even violence, often because of their verbal attacks on the brewing industry.

The Army spread overseas in 1880, first in the USA, then in Canada and India. Now it is found in over 90 countries, and has about two million members. In the UK, it has about 55,000 members in over 800 corps. In the Salvation Army Act of 1980, their aim is stated as 'The advancement of the Christian religion . . . of education, the relief of poverty, and other charitable objects beneficial to society'. The International Headquarters is in London.

Their military organisation

The overall leader is still the General, but is now elected by the High Council, which consists of commanders and other leading officers. Although the General has full authority to make decisions affecting the work of the Army, he or she has an Advisory Council and an International Management Council to help in shaping policy. Each of the territories has a territorial leader, responsible to the General. Territories have divisions, each with a commander.

The local corps (churches), which meet at the citadel, are led by commissioned (ordained) full-time, paid corps officers, who may be lieutenants or captains. They do not usually stay more than a few years in one place, and can be sent to any part of the world at short notice. Lay people with leadership responsibilities are known as local officers, the chief one being the corps sergeant-major. Women have always enjoyed equal rights with men, every rank and service being open to them. Many have done pioneer work.

To become a soldier (member), it is necessary first of all to sign the Articles of War, a statement of beliefs and promises. This includes a profession of personal salvation; a pledge of separation from the world and of loyalty to

Jesus Christ; and a pledge of allegiance to the Army, which is principally expressed by unquestioning obedience to the officers. Total abstinence from alcohol, drugs and tobacco is expected. Uniforms are worn by the soldiers.

Their teaching

The official statement of belief is clearly evangelical (p. 10) and Arminian (p. 12). It includes the following: '. . . that the Scriptures of the Old and New Testaments were given by inspiration of God and that they only constitute the Divine rule of Christian faith and practice; that the Lord Jesus Christ has by His sufferings and death made an atonement for the whole world so that whosoever will may be saved; that continuance in a state of salvation depends upon continued obedient faith in Christ'. Thus they have a strong emphasis on human free will, and believe that Christians can lose their salvation through moral and spiritual failure.

Holiness teaching along the lines of John Wesley's (p. 12) has always been prominent, so that an experience subsequent to conversion should be sought. 'We believe that it is the privilege of all believers to be wholly sanctified . . .'

They are quite clear about life after death: 'We believe in the immortality of the soul; in the resurrection of the body; in the general judgment at the end of the world; in the eternal happiness of the righteous; and in the endless punishment of the wicked.'

Neither baptism nor communion services are held, as it is believed that they are only symbols of spiritual truth. William Booth said they were not essential for salvation, and have often proved divisive. He said that 'at every meal they should remember that Christ's body was broken for their salvation'. They hold dedication services for children.

No set forms are laid down for worship, and spontaneity is encouraged. Singing plays a large part, accompanied by the band with songsters or choir. Preaching at some services is about holiness of life; at others, it is evangelistic.

A criticism used to be made that the officers were not given sufficient training in theology, and that too much emphasis was placed on experience. But now more academic training is being given. In recent years, a charismatic influence has become increasingly strong.

Their funeral services are quite joyful. They look upon death as being 'promoted to Glory', and feel it is wrong for Christians to feel 'mournful', even though there is a sense of loss.

Their method

Their main aim is evangelistic, to reach people for Christ. Open-air meetings are regularly held, accompanied by brass bands. Their newspaper, *The War Cry*, is distributed in public houses. But they have always believed that social and humanitarian work is necessary, to show the love of Christ in practice.

Thus, amongst many other things, they provide hostels for the homeless, rehabilitation units for alcoholics, and homes for the elderly, for maladjusted children, and for unmarried mothers; they do prison visitation, and help discharged prisoners; they provide a Missing Persons Bureau with many thousands of enquiries being dealt with each year; they arrange holidays and outings for the needy. Goodwill Centres are located in poorer areas of large cities, and smaller centres for men and women are now provided in many towns and cities.

Although their social work has been greatly admired, some friendly observers have said that today they do not always have the fire in preaching the gospel which was once so characteristic.

In recent years, they have played a bigger part in inter-church activities, especially in evangelism.

Seventh-Day Adventists

It is still very common for the Seventh-Day Adventists to be treated as being outside orthodox Christianity. Some writers have labelled them a cult. It is true that some of their doctrines have a very distinctive edge. And some of their writers have held views that could not be described as orthodox, even on major doctrines. In fact, there has been considerable turmoil over the years about their official teaching. It was not clear.

However, in 1995 they produced a *Statement of Fundamental Beliefs*, which was accepted by their 56th World Session. This leaves little doubt that on all the major issues of doctrine they are in line with mainstream Christianity. They would point out that most denominations have had preachers and writers who have had unusual, idiosyncratic views. And in the history of Seventh-Day Adventism, it is those views which critics have passed on as official teaching. Now it is clear where they stand – orthodox on major doctrines, but with some secondary doctrines all their own.

Their history

In the middle of the nineteenth century, there was much speculation about the Second Coming of Christ, particularly in the United States. William Miller, an American Baptist minister, prophesied it would take place by October 1844. After 'the great disappointment' (as it came to be described), certain revelations were received, so it was said, giving a new interpretation of the whole matter. People met to discuss these revelations. The writings of Mrs Ellen G. White (1827–1915) were particularly influential. In 1860, a conference was held when the name 'Seventh-Day Adventist' was first used, and the denomination was formed in 1863.

Regarded with great suspicion by the mainline denominations because of their unusual views, they were often portrayed as fanatics. So they retreated into their shell and went their own way,

Missionary work became a great priority. Now they are in most parts of the world, working in 209 countries. Although often thought of as an American movement, less than 10% of their worldwide membership of 8 million is in North America. They started in Britain in 1878, where they now have about 19,000 members.

In many areas of the world, they run schools and hospitals, and have one of the biggest international relief agencies — ADRA, the Adventist Development and Relief Agency. This is active in nearly 100 countries, providing all kinds of humanitarian aid. They also run radio stations and have their own publishing house.

Their teaching

The Bible is accepted as the infallible Word of God, and the only rule for faith and conduct. In the past, critics have maintained that they count the writings of Ellen G. White as having the same authority as the Bible. Some Adventists seem to have done so. Now the official line is that her writings are simply a commentary on the Bible. It is made clear that the Bible is the standard by which all teaching and experiences must be tested.

Orthodox teaching about the Trinity is upheld – 'a unity of three co-eternal Persons'.

They have been accused of believing that Christ had a sinful nature when he was here on earth. Some Adventist writings may seem to have suggested this. However, their view is that Christ 'perfectly exemplified the righteousness and love of God'; his life was 'of perfect obedience to God's will'.

Critics have also said that Adventists believe that Christ's work of atonement on the cross was not complete. Again, some Adventist writers have suggested this. But the official statement speaks of Christ's 'perfect atonement ... the only means of atonement for human sin ... the death of Christ is substitutionary and expiatory.'

Some evangelical critics have accused them of not believing fully in 'justification by faith'. This, to a large extent, is because of the way the Adventists insist that Christians should keep the law of the Old Testament. This again is a misunderstanding. The statement says:

> Led by the Holy Spirit, we sense our need, acknowledge our sinfulness, repent of our transgressions, and exercise faith in Jesus as Lord and Christ, as Substitute and Example. This faith which receives salvation comes through the divine power of the Word and is the gift of God's grace. Through Christ we are justified, adopted as God's sons and daughters, and delivered from the lordship of sin. Salvation is all of grace and not of works, but its fruitage is obedience to the Commandments. This obedience develops Christian character and results in a sense of well-being.

Another criticism has been that they considered themselves to be the only true Church of God. In fact, their statement now makes it clear that 'the Church is the community of believers who confess Jesus Christ as Lord and Saviour'.

There are ways in which they differ from most other churches:

(a) *The Sabbath.* The outstanding doctrine is that the seventh day of the week must be kept as the Sabbath and the day of worship. As one of the Ten Commandments, it must be observed literally. As with the Jews, the Sabbath runs from sunset Friday to sunset Saturday. They do not believe, as has sometimes been said, that keeping the Sabbath is necessary for salvation, or that 'the mark of the beast' is on those who keep Sundays. But they believe the Bible teaches that the Lord's Day of the New Testament is the same as the Sabbath of the Old Testament. They state categorically that creation took place in six days, and then God rested on the seventh day. 'Thus He established the Sabbath as a perpetual memorial of His completed creative work.'

(b) *Soul sleep.* Although believing in the Second Coming of Christ, there is no question of saying when it might happen. As premillennialists (p. 14), they believe it could happen at any time. But their belief is that when Christians die, their soul is not active at all. It sleeps in the grave, being unconscious until the resurrection day. When Christ returns, the righteous dead and living will both be taken to heaven, where they will reign with Christ for a thousand years. During this time, the earth will be desolate, occupied only by Satan and his angels. At the end of the thousand years, Christ will return to earth with his saints; the wicked will be resurrected; the final battle will take place; and afterwards, Satan and the unrighteous will not suffer eternal torment, but be annihilated. The universe will then be freed from sin and sinners for ever.

(c) *The final work of Christ.* They believe that Christ began the final part of his work in 1844 (the time of the 'great disappointment'). His work on the cross was complete in atoning for sin, but until 1844, 'sins still remained on the book of record'. It was now that Christ began his 'investigative judgment', deciding those who will take part in the resurrection of believers and who will not. Salvation can be lost because of disobedience or turning away from Christ. They believe that the Old Testament cleansing of the sanctuary on the Day of Atonement is a symbolic picture of what Christ is doing now.

Satan, as the originator of all sin, will have to suffer the punishment due for all the sins that have been committed. In this sense, he is the scapegoat of Leviticus 16. This does not mean he makes atonement for sin (which some critics have said they teach).

Some Adventists have disputed the teaching on the investigative judgment, keeping to the traditional teaching that Christ continues to intercede for his people until his Second Coming.

Their organisation

At all levels, they operate a committee system. All action and policies must pass through a committee stage before being put into practice.

For the UK, a Union Conference operates at national level in England, but missions operate in Ireland, Scotland and Wales.

In the local church, officers, including pastors, are nominated by a committee and then voted upon by the church members.

The final authority for faith and practice is the General Conference Session of the worldwide Church, which meets every five years.

Church life

Worship services tend to be exuberant, with rousing singing, clapping and congregational participation. This is largely because of black immigration since the 1950s. Now less than a quarter of the membership is white. A move to recruit more white members is under way, with some preferring a more reserved style of worship. Choirs play an important part in the worship.

Baptism is for believers only and is by immersion. It follows an affirmation of faith in Christ and evidence of repentance from sin. It leads to membership in the church.

The Lord's Supper, the Communion service, is held regularly and 'is open to all believing Christians'. They use unleavened bread and unfermented wine.

They believe in spiritual gifts such as healing and prophecy. For them, Ellen G. White had the gift of prophecy.

Members are expected to give at least a tenth of their income, and to abstain from alcohol, tobacco and drugs. They must live up to the highest moral standards and to dress modestly. The Church runs health food shops, and the need for a healthy diet is constantly being stressed.

United Reformed Church

The Church was formed in 1972 when the English Presbyterian Church united with the English Congregational Church. The Churches of Christ joined in 1981. The 'formation and growth' of the Church is seen 'as a part of what God is doing to make his people one, and as a united Church will take, wherever possible and with all speed, further steps towards the unity of all God's people'.

The URC has a presbyterian form of church government (p. 7). The highest authority for faith and practice is the General Assembly, which has an equal number of ministerial and lay representatives, and certain special representatives, up to a total of 750.

England and Wales are divided into 12 Provinces, each with a Moderator, who exercises pastoral oversight of the churches and ministry. The Provinces are subdivided into Districts. District Councils, which are largely made up of all ministers and representative elders from the churches, have much responsibility for the ministers and churches. They accredit lay preachers.

Local churches

These are run by the elders' meeting, made up of ministers (who can be men or women), auxiliary ministers (those who are not paid), and elders, who are elected by the members of the church. A church meeting of members is held four times a year to consider the life of the church. Each congregation has freedom to develop its own patterns of worship and mission, and it is they who accept candidates for membership. A minister can be called by the church meeting, as long as the district council agrees. Some ministers are responsible for more than one congregation. Each elder is ordained, and has a group of members to care for.

Admission to membership follows a public profession of faith, and baptism. Both infant and believers' baptism are recognised. But, in either case, baptism 'is the sacrament of entry into the Church, and is therefore administered once only to any person'. Ministers usually preside at baptisms and the Lord's Supper, but lay people can be given authority to do so by the District Council. However, 'no one shall be required to administer a form or mode of baptism to which he has a conscientious objection'.

Worship services vary quite widely in their content. Some hold to traditional forms, with the minister leading the prayers and Bible readings, and preaching the sermon. Some are more free, some 'charismatic' (p. 16), with modern songs being sung, and participation by members of the congregation.

Their teaching

In *The Faith of the United Reformed Church*, the Bible is acknowledged 'as the supreme authority for the faith and conduct of all God's people'. At the same time, they accept the historic creeds, and recognise 'as its own particular heritage the formulations and declarations of faith which have been valued by Congregationalists, Presbyterians and members of Churches of Christ'. These are the Westminster Confession, the Savoy Declaration and Thomas Campbell's Declaration and Address.

The Church 'upholds the rights of personal conviction'. But the confession of faith is in 'the one living and true God, creator, preserver and ruler of all things in heaven and earth, Father, Son and Holy Spirit'. Jesus Christ

> died upon the Cross for our sins, rose again from the dead and lives for evermore, saviour, judge and king. By the Holy Spirit, this glorious gospel is made effective so that through faith we receive the forgiveness of sins, newness of life as children of God and strength in this present world to do his will. By the same Spirit, the whole company of believers is made one Body of Christ. In the fulness of time, God will renew and gather in one all things in Christ. There is also now an Alternative Statement of Faith, which has a more liberal slant.

An issue being warmly debated is whether homosexuals can be ordained to the ministry. Some people believe that the denomination could be split over the matter. At present, no firm ruling has been laid down, only that the local churches must decide for themselves. A church can ordain and appoint a homosexual minister if they so wish, although, as always, the choice must be upheld by the district council. But many in the denomination feel the whole policy is wrong.

Membership is over 100,000 in some 1750 churches.

GEAR

The Group for Evangelism and Renewal came into being in 1974, because it was felt there was a need to offset the liberal (p. 9) theology in the denomination by bringing together those who had an evangelical (p. 10) theology, who wanted to 'foster the renewal of the Church in the

Holy Spirit', and in order 'to encourage participation in forms of outreach relevant to today'.

GEAR does not have a membership, and aims 'to be a servant to the whole Church'. But it is generally recognised as representing many of those who are evangelical and charismatic in the URC. Some of the GEAR committee serve on the national, provincial and district committees of the URC. Conferences are held and literature published.

They have their own statement of faith. Although not disagreeing with the URC Statement of Faith, they feel the need to go further, e.g. by affirming that the Bible is 'God's written Word, inspired by his Spirit', by which God has made himself 'explicitly' known. They declare the virgin birth of Jesus, and that he 'will return visibly and personally', when he 'will pronounce God's just condemnatiom on those who have rejected him and receive the redeemed to eternal glory'.

REAM

More recently, another group has been formed, an Evangelical Association of Ministers within the Reformed tradition, known as REAM. Many of these ministers are also in GEAR. But because GEAR has no official membership, it was felt a complementary Association was necessary to represent a particular URC constituency especially in the Evangelical Alliance, whose statement of faith they endorse.

REAM does not organise conferences or issue a regular newsletter. It is a network of evangelical ministers already in the EA, to provide supportive fellowship and to work together on theological issues with evangelicals in the wider church.

Vineyard Churches

The Vineyard movement began in America in the late 1970s through John Wimber. It now works in over 30 countries, with about 600 churches. Although John Wimber became well known in Britain during the '80s, Vineyard churches only started here in 1987. Now they have nearly 50 churches, and more are continually being added. Some churches of other denominations have close links with the Association of Vineyard Churches.

Their theology is evangelical (p. 10) and charismatic (p. 16), but with an emphasis that 'signs and wonders', wrought by the Holy Spirit, should be seen in connection with evangelism as well as within the local church. They believe this was the pattern in the New Testament. As people see the power of God, they are more ready to listen to the word of God.

So they teach the need for Christians to be baptised in the Holy Spirit, and that, in the kingdom of God, there can be dominion over illness and Satan. They believe that the Bible is 'without error in the original manuscripts', and receive it as the 'final, absolute authority, the only infallible rule of faith and practice'. But they also believe that God has his 'current prophetic word', which needs to be heard.

Church life

Churches are run by pastors, who are given authority to make final decisions, after consultation. Although churches are autonomous, area pastoral co-ordinators guide the pastors and help to give oversight to the churches. Trained personnel are sent on short-term ministry trips to the churches, and also help to plant new churches.

Churches do not have a membership as such. The ethos is that relationships are the key to church life. All who come are expected to join a house group, and training is given to equip them for some kind of Christian service. Strict moral standards are laid down, and reproof must be accepted. They are also expected to give generously, and 'care for the poor and those in need'. A high priority is given to humanitarian work, such as helping prisoners and feeding the homeless.

Baptism is only for believers. The Lord's Supper (Communion) is held regularly. In their worship, they try to be as culturally sensitive as possible. Their words and music are in a contemporary style.

Wesleyan Reform Union

The Union started life in 1849, when three ministers and many other members were expelled from, or decided to leave, the Wesleyan Methodist Church. They had been agitating for reform for some time, especially with regard to church government. Their great belief was in the independency of the local church, that each has the right to administer its own affairs. So the Wesleyan Reform Union of Churches was founded.

Although the churches are organised into circuits, all of them are autonomous. Full authority is vested in the members' meeting. The Union holds an annual conference, with delegates from the circuits and certain individual churches. It is not involved with the ecumenical movement, but does work closely with the Countess of Huntingdon's Connexion and the Independent Methodists. At local level, there is much co-operation with other churches, and social action is undertaken.

The 120 churches are nearly all in England, and the membership is nearly 2500. The headquarters is in Sheffield. Although many churches have ministers, the accredited local (lay) preachers are able to function as ministers, including the administration of baptism and the Lord's Supper. Baptism is reserved only for believers.

The theology of the Union is strongly evangelical (p. 10). Some churches have a 'charismatic' (p. 16) emphasis. The Confession of Faith includes: 'The Holy Scriptures, both Old and New Testaments, as originally given, are of divine inspiration and infallible, supreme in authority in all matters of faith and practice. The Holy Spirit . . . indwells every believer as his Sanctifier, thus placing His seal upon him as a child of God.'

PART 3

Non-Trinitarian Churches

Under this heading come some of the many groups which may call themselves Christian, but which deny the kind of teaching considered vital in orthodox Christianity, substituting instead their own doctrine. This particularly involves their understanding about Jesus in his relationship to God, and what he accomplished on the cross. It involves their understanding of salvation, what it means and how it is brought about. None of them believes in the Trinity as traditionally taught.

They believe they have been given special revelation by God to account for their teaching. This may be in addition to the Bible, or a new interpretation of it. This has usually come to one individual, who has a great ability to attract followers. They tend to be highly organised, have a strong commitment to one another, and often expect submission to authority. They keep themselves separate from other groups, believing they have all the truth that is needed — they alone are the true Church.

Some have links with Eastern Religions, some believe they are able to link all religions, some claim to have a new understanding of the Bible message. Most have arisen during the last 150 years or so, many during the last 40 years.

A number of cults or religious groups call themselves 'Churches'. Here are the main points of the teaching of some of them.

Christian Science Churches

Christian Science was founded by Mary Baker Eddy (1821–1910) in Massachusetts, USA. Her book, *Science and Health with Key to the Scriptures* is seen as having at least the same authority as the Bible. Mrs Eddy said that many biblical statements were wrong. Basic to her teaching is her denial of the existence of matter, pain, evil and death. They only seem to exist because mankind is under the spell of 'mortal Mind', a perverted human understanding. In reality there is only Mind. God is Mind or Principle. 'Life, Truth and Love constitute the triune person called God, that is, the triply divine Principle Love.'

'Jesus is the human man, and Christ the divine idea.' Sin is only an illusion of the mind, and does not need the sacrifice of Christ. In fact, Jesus did not die.

'Heaven is not a reality, but a state of mind.' 'Hell is mortal belief, self-imposed agony.'

The main concern is with physical healing. Mrs Eddy believed she had restored the power of healing which had been lost since the days of the New Testament. 'What is termed disease does not exist.' The apparent reality must be denied. Even death is an illusion. 'Mortals waken from the dream of death with bodies unseen by those who think that they bury the body.'

It is often said that Christian Science is neither Christian nor scientific because for them, God is not personal, Jesus is not God, evil does not exist, the death of Christ was not necessary, neither is a spiritual salvation, and heaven is only a state of mind.

Church of Jesus Christ of Latter-Day Saints (Mormons)

The Church was founded by Joseph Smith (1805–44). He claimed that, when he was 17, he had a vision. An angelic messenger, called Moroni, told him where to find some golden plates, hidden in a hill. The writing on the plates was in ancient Egyptian hieroglyphics, which he would be able to translate with the help of two crystals, the Urim and the Thummim, a kind of spectacles. This, he said, he did. The translation is called *The Book of Mormon*, first published in 1830.

The Church's headquarters is at Salt Lake City, Utah, USA. They believe the Bible to be the word of God 'as far as it is translated correctly'. They also believe the *Book of Mormon* to be the word of God, which contains revelation not available to those who wrote the Bible.

The teaching is that God has a body with flesh and bones. He is really an exalted man. All human beings can become as God is now, although he himself will go ever higher.

Jesus Christ had a 'unique status in the flesh as the offspring of a mortal mother (Mary) and an immortal, or resurrected and glorified, Father (Elohim)'.

The Holy Spirit is 'the third personage of the Godhead', but cannot be in more than one place at a time.

For salvation, there must be not only faith in Christ, but 'the laws and ordinances of the Gospel' must be kept. These include the Mormon observances. Baptism by immersion is essential. Those living now can be baptized on behalf of dead relatives, who were not able to have a Mormon baptism.

Their Church is alone the true church, with the true gospel restored. All other churches are false. Soon Christ will return. He will establish his kingdom in America, the new Jerusalem, which is why those living overseas are encouraged to emigrate there. This kingdom will last a thousand years, and Mormons will preach to those considered worthy to live then. Following this, there will be the second resurrection and final judgment. It would seem that eventually all human beings will be in heaven, but only Mormons will reach the highest grade, Celestial Glory.

Thus, their teaching is at odds with almost every foundational doctrine of mainline Christianity. Although they say they 'believe in God, his Son Jesus Christ and in the Holy Ghost', in fact their conception is of three Gods, physically separate from each other. They also say that every human being is a potential god, but only if they are Mormons.

Jehovah's Witnesses

Although the Witnesses do not call themselves a Church that is how they see themselves, that in fact they are the true descendants of the New Testament church. Founded by C.T. Russell in 1874, the International Headquarters is in Brooklyn, New York. Almost total authority is in the hands of the governing body, who are seen as God's channel for truth today. Throughout the world, meetings at each Kingdom Hall study the same subjects through *The Watchtower* magazine sent out from Brooklyn.

Members do not vote in elections or fight for their country. They cannot have blood transfusions, believing this to be against Bible teaching.

All other religious leaders, churches and organisations are described as false, deceived and controlled by Satan. Their own translation of the Bible is the *New World Translation*, but to be interpreted properly, it is necessary to use *The Watchtower* magazine.

The doctrine of the Trinity is described as being inspired by Satan. The Holy Spirit is not a Person, only God's active force. Christ was the first creation of Jehovah, who had existed alone from eternity. He, Christ, is not God, only a 'mighty being'. Before being born as Jesus, he was the archangel Michael. As Jesus, he was no longer a spirit-being, but a perfect human being. After his resurrection, he returned to being a spirit-being, no longer having a human body.

When Jesus died, he paid to God the ransom price necessary to set human beings free from death caused by Adam's sin, and gave them an opportunity to earn eternal life. This can only be merited as Jehovah is accepted and his will obeyed, as taught by the Witnesses.

Christ returned to earth invisibly as a spirit-being in 1914. Soon the last great battle, Armageddon, will take place, followed by the Millennium. During the thousand years, those who have not opposed the Jehovah's Witnesses teaching will be given a second chance. Afterwards, all who have rejected the teaching will be annihilated.

So, their teaching is unorthodox and false, because of the denial of the Trinity, and because salvation must be earned by good works, involving loyalty to Jehovah's Witnesses and declaring their teaching to others.

New Church or Swedenborgianism

Its full name is 'The Church of the New Jerusalem', and it follows the teaching of Emmanuel Swedenborg (1688–1772). He was a distinguished scientist, engineer and inventor, a Professor at the University of Uppsala in Sweden. He left this life behind in 1745, saying he had been called to concentrate on spiritual truth. He claimed to have received new revelation from God.

He accepted only parts of the Bible as being inspired — 29 books of the Old Testament, and five of the New (the four Gospels and Revelation). He strongly denied there was a Trinity. God is an infinite man, existing in perfect human form, 'the eternal God-Man'.

At the incarnation, the one God was born of Mary, 'assuming a material body with its physical life'. The cross was not a sacrifice for sin, but a 'subjugation of the powers of evil'. There was not a bodily resurrection of Christ, only a gradual refining of his body until it was lost in the spiritual and eternal.

He disagreed that salvation comes by faith alone. It comes by repentance, when forgiveness is received. Everybody has the ability to live a good and loving life, and can choose to do so. After death, we enter the realm of the spirits, and become either an angel in heaven or an evil spirit in hell. There is no bodily resurrection in the future, or judgment. The Last Judgment took place in 1757. Since then, there has been a new dispensation, based on the truths revealed to Swedenborg. The other churches must, in time, give way to the Church of the New Jerusalem.

Again, it is one man putting forward his own views, disagreeing with the Bible and the teaching of mainline churches.

Church of Scientology

This Church was founded in 1954 by L. Ron Hubbard (1911–86). He was an American, who had been a science fiction writer. In 1950, he had published his book, *Dianetics: The Modern Science of Mental Health*, which now became the textbook of the movement.

Critics have often questioned its right to be called a church. It uses very little religious terminology, although Sunday services are held, and they have their own rites of baptism, marriage and funerals.

Hubbard saw his work as an extension of the work of Buddha, and was also inspired by the Vedic Hymns of Hinduism. He said that Scientology was a programme to 'revolutionise character, give more sense of purpose, get rid of tensions and inhibitions'. This is brought about by increasing knowledge of oneself.

Mankind is basically good, but has been affected by unpleasant experiences in the past, in previous lives as well as this one. These are recorded in the subconscious as 'engrams'. If nothing is done, they lead to psychological disorders. Through the 'processing' procedures of Dianetics, for which fees are paid, there can be increasing release from engrams.

The ultimate aim, through many 'grades', is to become an 'operating thetan' (pronounce thaitan). A thetan is basically the person himself — not his body or his name — but the identity which is the individual. The potential of this immortal spirit is massive. Neither Buddha nor Jesus Christ were operating thetans. They had only reached part of the way.

Scientology is more psychology than anything else. There is no real Christian doctrine; the Bible is only one of many 'holy' books; God is hardly mentioned; Christ is only a respected teacher. Repentance is not necessary, because man is not evil. Freedom from the cycle of birth and death (reincarnation) comes only through self-masterly, attained through Scientology, and, they claim, leads to control over matter, energy, space and time.

Spiritualist Church

The basis of their teaching is that it is possible to communicate with the spirits of people who have died. This will usually be through a medium, or 'sensitive' as they are sometimes called. At a seance, the medium's body is taken over by a 'control spirit', a 'spirit-guide', who can guide to other spirits with whom contact is desired. Sometimes it is the spirit from 'the other side' who wants to get in touch. Voices may be heard, forms and faces may be seen and objects may move.

Answers to questions may be given with the spirit's voice coming from the medium's mouth, through the ouija board or tarot cards, or through 'automatic writing'. It is claimed that, in this way, certainty can be given about where loved ones are, and if they are happy. It gives assurance that life continues after death. It is also said that healings take place.

Most Spiritualist churches belong either to The Spiritualists' National Union or The Greater World Christian Spiritualist League.

It is acknowledged by themselves that much fraud and deception has taken place. But independent investigations have shown that unusual happenings do take place. Many critics would say these are due to evil spirits, who can impersonate dead people.

Although considering themselves a branch of Christianity, they do not accept the inspiration of the Bible. They say the teaching against mediums, etc. in the Old Testament, e.g. in Deuteronomy 18, is really against imposters. But in fact, it does not say that, and it is made very clear that there must be no attempt at all to make contact with the spirits of dead people, and that all mediums are 'detested' by God.

God is described by them as Infinite Intelligence. Jesus is called the supreme medium, with outstanding sensitivity in the spiritual realm. The cross simply shows his martyr spirit.

Everyone has a 'spark of divinity'. Nobody is naturally bad. Evil always originates in ignorance. Forgiveness is not needed through the cross. We make our own happiness or unhappiness by the way we live.

After death, everybody goes to 'the other side', however they may have lived. Neither heaven nor hell exists. The spirit leaves the physical body, with no change of personality or loss of memory. It can now progress in a place which is much happier and more beautiful, but otherwise very similar to this world.

Spiritualism can only be described as a great deception and very dangerous.

Unification Church

This Church is often known as 'The Moonies' after the founder, Sun Myung Moon, 'Shining Sun and Moon'. It began in 1954 in Seoul, Korea. The headquarters now is in New York State. The main textbook is *Divine Principle*, written by one of Mr Moon's followers in 1957. It is claimed that this is God's latest revelation as given to Mr Moon. It takes precedence over the Bible, which is seen as imperfect.

The teaching is that, when God first made man, he wanted him to establish a perfect family. But sin came in when Eve had sexual relations with Lucifer, as well as with Adam. This resulted in both a spiritual and physical fall, needing a physical as well as a spiritual salvation.

The mission of Jesus was meant to accomplish this salvation by marrying and setting up a perfect family with sinless children. This would bring about the kingdom of heaven on earth. But he failed to do this, not getting married, and allowing himself to be crucified, so giving a victory to Satan. By his resurrection 'as a spirit', he only accomplished a partial 'spiritual' salvation.

To bring 'physical' salvation, God would have to send a new Messiah, fulfilling the prophecies about the Second Coming. He would establish a perfect family, and lead the armies of God against Satan as 'Lord of the Second Advent'.

Mr Moon is this Messiah. It is claimed that everybody will eventually join the Unification Church, and so be brought back to God. It will be heaven on earth. Followers are encouraged to break family ties and live at one of the Church's centres. They can only be safe there. Their sins, and those of their ancestors, must be atoned for by continual activity.

Because the family is so vital in the kingdom of heaven, members submit a list of five possible marriage partners. Leaders make the final choice. Divorce is only possible when one partner leaves the Church.

Unification teaching uplifts one man in the place of Christ. The New Testament declares Christ as the only Messiah and Saviour both spiritually and physically, through his death and resurrection. He did not fail, and it is he who is going to return as King of kings and Lord of lords.

Unitarian Church

Since the early days of Christianity, there have been people who have maintained the basic Unitarian beliefs, which were condemned by the mainstream churches. It was only after the Reformation that churches were formed to promote this teaching. Essex Chapel, London was founded in 1774. Most Unitarian churches are in the USA. In the UK, churches belong to the General Assembly of Unitarian and Free Christian Churches, formed in 1928.

Freedom, reason and tolerance are vital. The Bible is only one of many divine books, and must be interpreted according to reason. The historic creeds are rejected, along with belief in the atonement through the cross, the bodily resurrection of Jesus and his return, with final judgment. Jesus was a good man and a great example, who died as a martyr.

People are essentially good, and salvation is 'by character'. No mediator is necessary to approach God. Heaven and hell do not exist. Good will finally triumph over evil.

At the heart of their teaching is the denial of the Trinity. God does not exist in three Persons, only in one. Christ and the Holy Spirit are not members of the Godhead. The name Unitarian expresses God's unipersonality.

Worldwide Church of God

In recent years, a revolution has taken place in the official teaching of this church. It could be that, in time, it will be accepted as having orthodox teaching, at least as far as the major doctrines are concerned. It has already been accepted as a member of the National Evangelical Alliance in the USA.

The Church was founded in 1934 by Herbert W. Armstrong (1892–1986). The headquarters are in California, and it operates in 120 countries. The magazine *The Plain Truth* has become well known.

Armstrong's key emphasis was that God is making people literally like himself, so that they will be gods. Salvation is a process. 'Nobody is yet saved. The blood of Christ does not finally save any man. The death of Christ merely paid the penalty of sin in our stead – it saves us from the death penalty – it removes that which separates us from God.' But 'it is only those who . . . have developed spiritually, done the works of Christ and endured to the end, who shall finally be given immortality at the Second Coming of Christ'.

When somebody repents and puts their faith in Christ, they are 'impregnated with the life of God'. They are conceived, but not born again. Now they must keep all the laws of the Bible. This means, for example, being baptised, keeping Saturday as the Sabbath, not eating pork, etc. etc. Then they will be born again when Christ returns, and become divine. 'Jesus, alone, of all humans, has so far been saved.'

Armstrong was succeeded by Joseph Tkach, who initiated the immense changes which have taken place since 1986. He died in 1995, but in that year a new Statement of Beliefs was issued.

The Trinity is now clearly taught, along with the bodily resurrection of Jesus. They still worship on Saturdays, but Sabbath-keeping is not necessary for salvation, which is only 'by grace'. 'Salvation is the gift of God, by grace through faith in Jesus Christ, not earned by personal merit or works.' Christians are those who are born again now by the Holy Spirit. The Worldwide Church of God is not exclusively the Body of Christ.

Because the Church has changed so much, membership has fallen. Some have left altogether. Some have joined the Philadelphia Church of God, founded in 1989 with the express purpose of maintaining Armstrong's teaching. Amongst those who have remained in the Church, many are confused. Inevitably it will take time for changes to be accepted by ordinary members. It is a time of much uncertainty.

Some Further Reading

Introducing the Apostolic Church (Apostolic Publications)

The Baptists in Scotland, ed. D.W. Bebbington (Baptist Union of Scotland)

The Origins of the Brethren, H.H. Rowden (Marshall Pickering)

The New Catechism of the Roman Catholic Church (Jeffrey Chapman)

The Church and Its Unity, ed. Alan Gibson (IVP) Reflecting different opinions about the church amongst Evangelicals.

Reaffirming the Church of England, Hugh Montefiore (Triangle) Simple Guide.

From Controversy to Co-existence, Randle Manwaring (CUP) The Church of England.

The Anglican Evangelical Crisis, ed. Melvin Tinker (Christian Focus Publications) The Reform Group states their case.

Who are the Evangelicals? Derek J. Tidball (Marshall Pickering)

For Such a Time as This, ed. Steve Brady and Harold Rowden (Scripture Union) Where Evangelicals are heading.

Fire in Our Hearts, Simon Cooper and Mike Farrant (Kingsway) The story of the Jesus Fellowship.

The Kingdom of the Cults, Walter Martin (Bethany House Publishers) An excellent study of the Non-Trinitarian Movements, but comes out strongly on behalf of the Seventh Day Adventists.

Messianic Jews, John Fieldsend (Monarch Publications)

Doing a New Thing, Brian Hewitt (Hodder and Stoughton) Interviews with leaders of New Churches, the House Church Movement.

Restoring the Kingdom, Andrew Walker (Hodder and Stoughton) An indepth study of the House Church Movement, now somewhat out of date.

The Pentecostals, W. Hollenweger (SCM) A good survey of the whole Pentecostal Movement throughout the world.

Christianity: A World Faith (Lion Publishing) Reflects the world-wide kaleidoscope of Christian faith today.

Evangelica & Congregational (Evangelical Fellowship of Congregational Churches) Principles of the Congregational Independence.